On Agamben, Arendt, Christianity, and the Dark Arts of Civilization

READING AUGUSTINE

Series editor

Miles Hollingworth

Reading Augustine offers personal and close readings of St. Augustine of Hippo from leading philosophers and religious scholars. Its aim is to make clear Augustine's importance to contemporary thought and to present Augustine not only or primarily as a preeminent Christian thinker but as a philosophical, spiritual, literary, and intellectual icon of the West.

Volumes in the series

On Ethics, Politics and Psychology in the Twenty-First Century, John Rist

On Love, Confession, Surrender and the Moral Self, Ian Clausen

On Education, Formation, Citizenship and the Lost Purpose of Learning, Joseph Clair

On Creativity, Liberty, Love and the Beauty of the Law, Todd Breyfogle

On Consumer Culture, Identity, the Church and the Rhetorics of Delight, Mark Clavier

On God, the Soul, Evil and the Rise of Christianity, John Peter Kenney

On Music, Sound, Affect and Ineffability, Carol Harrison

On Self-Harm, Narcissism, Atonement and the Vulnerable Christ, David Vincent Meconi

On Agamben, Arendt, Christianity, and the Dark Arts of Civilization

Peter Iver Kaufman

BLOOMSBURY ACADEMIC
LONDON • NEW YORK • OXFORD • NEW DELHI • SYDNEY

BLOOMSBURY ACADEMIC
Bloomsbury Publishing Plc
50 Bedford Square, London, WC1B 3DP, UK
1385 Broadway, New York, NY 10018, USA

BLOOMSBURY, BLOOMSBURY ACADEMIC and the DIANA logo are trademarks of Bloomsbury Publishing Plc

First published in Great Britain 2020

Copyright © Peter Iver Kaufman, 2020

Peter Iver Kaufman has asserted his right under the Copyright, Designs and Patents Act, 1988, to be identified as Author of this work.

For legal purposes the Acknowledgments on p. vi constitute an extension of this copyright page.

Series design by Catherine Wood
Cover image: St. Laurent du Maroni, statue of a prisoner
© W2C TM Multimedia – Travel Pictures Gallery 2019. French Guiana pictures.

All rights reserved. No part of this publication may be reproduced or transmitted in any form or by any means, electronic or mechanical, including photocopying, recording, or any information storage or retrieval system, without prior permission in writing from the publishers.

Bloomsbury Publishing Plc does not have any control over, or responsibility for, any third-party websites referred to or in this book. All internet addresses given in this book were correct at the time of going to press. The author and publisher regret any inconvenience caused if addresses have changed or sites have ceased to exist, but can accept no responsibility for any such changes.

A catalogue record for this book is available from the British Library.

A catalog record for this book is available from the Library of Congress.

ISBN: HB: 978-0-5676-8277-2
PB: 978-0-5676-8275-8
ePDF: 978-0-5676-8278-9
ePUB: 978-0-5676-8281-9

Series: Reading Augustine

Typeset by Deanta Global Publishing Services, Chennai, India
Printed and bound in Great Britain

To find out more about our authors and books visit www.bloomsbury.com and sign up for our newsletters.

CONTENTS

Acknowledgments vi
Preface viii
Abbreviations: Augustine's Works xi

1   Augustine and Agamben 1
2   Glory, Glory 49
3   Arendt's Augustine 99

Further Reading 149
Index 152

ACKNOWLEDGMENTS

For three years I've been trying out the interpretations you'll find here. Faculty and student colleagues at the Universities of Virginia, Chicago, North Carolina, and Richmond as well as at Samford and Fordham Universities have been remarkably generous; their comments, questions, and, above all, criticisms have kept me thinking and rewriting. Chuck Mathewes, at the University of Virginia; Eric Gregory, at Princeton University, and Bob Dodaro, at the Institutum Patristicum Augustinianum, Rome, have been with me every step—inasmuch as their granite resolve to find resources in Augustine's "political theology" for what they variously call "hopeful citizenship," "democratic citizenship," and "the just society" in our messy political cultures continues to stir my resolve to find in Augustine resources for a much more radical alternative. I'm tremendously grateful that discussing our disagreements only deepens our friendships. And immensely helpful comments and encouragement from Ward Blanton, a former student and, now, faculty colleague at the University of Kent, Canterbury, marked a renewal of our friendship, for which I am thankful.

When I moved from a research (or R1) university to my current post at a relatively small liberal arts college, I feared that chasing down texts in their original languages—and much of the interpretive literature from Europe—would be challenging, if not impossible. But I was surprised. My new colleagues in the University of Richmond library—Lucretia McCulley, Sam Schuth, Travis Smith, Jalesa (Lese) Taylor, and Kimberly Wolfe—could not have been kinder or more resourceful. I cram their inbox with requests; they inspire me with their friendships, enthusiasm, and effectiveness. I'm clearly the beneficiary in this lopsided relationship. The preface will explain what I've written and, in part, why. But there'd be no "what" or "why" without them or without Miles Hollingworth, editor of the series, who said "write"—and, sometimes, "wrong."

Expressing confidence in the project from the start, he got its pulse racing with his every email, commenting insightfully on its trajectory and critically on its compass. This series is a tremendous tribute to Miles's ingenuity, and this volume is my thanks for his having risked letting a historian poach in political theory and cultural criticism.

The conceit here is that pilgrims, refugees, and pariahs have unique, useful perspectives on the socially and invidiously constructed concept of citizenship. Awareness of that has led this book's three principals to offer alternatives. Nearly twenty years ago—*before* I became aware of contributions Augustine, Arendt, and Agamben could make on this issue—University of North Carolina undergraduates and I organized the Scholars Latino Initiative (SLI) to assist undocumented high school students prepare to compete for admission to—and to survive in—colleges and universities. SLI has worked with several hundred high school students and has expanded. Virginia has three chapters. The students, undergraduate mentors, site directors, and our community partners compose what, given the political climate, has become an underground "railway" to higher education. These twenty years, they have taught me more about courage, perseverance, and resourcefulness than all I did and read during the previous fifty plus. They've taught me what to look for in Augustine, Arendt, and Agamben. Gratefully—affectionately—this book is dedicated to the SLI family.

PREFACE

Neither Augustine nor Giorgio Agamben seems to have interested Ari Adut—and his book's few references to Hannah Arendt suggest that he and I read her differently—but I suspect Augustine, Agamben, and Arendt would have endorsed the summary judgment of Adut's *Reign of Appearances*. Augustine, in the early fifth century; Arendt in the late 1950s and 1960s; and Agamben, recently—in their respective idioms—have anticipated Adut's assessment that "the public sphere is not the realm of civic dialogue, a deliberative order in which citizenship is exercised. It is simply a space of appearances . . . a spectacle." Adut is a shrewd, censorious student of "the facile exhibitionism" of "our confessional culture," where "publicity may bring out the courageous individualist [but] . . . will not fail to make cowardly conformists of countless others." So *Reign of Appearances* is no brief for what many political theorists think "essential to a well-functioning democracy": "a vibrant" public sphere, realm, or domain.[1]

In the 1960s, I came to doubt what those "many theorists" were and are thinking. I chose to study and teach medieval and early modern soteriology for years. It seemed to me then—and it seems now—a fine way to hibernate. In the late 1980s, John Wilson of Princeton University, my benefactor in many ways, asked me to contribute to his series, "Studies in Church and State," a book on religion and politics in the history of Christianity, *Redeeming Politics*.[2] My chapter on Augustine's political pessimism drew fire,

---

[1] Ari Adut, *Reign of Appearances: The Misery and Splendor of the Public Sphere* (Cambridge: Cambridge University Press, 2018), ix–x and 88. But Adut, although critical of political claims made for the "spectacle," concludes (146–57) with a brief for "spectatorship" and the aesthetic value of the public sphere.
[2] Peter Iver Kaufman, *Redeeming Politics* (Princeton: Princeton University Press, 1990).

but, aside from a few articles, I let the issue drop for over fifteen years and steered well clear of political theory until I had time to lodge Augustine's doubts about evangelizing the political order in a biographical study, which I docked beside a similar study of Thomas More, known to have lectured on Augustine. I tried to show how and why Augustine (and More) came to believe that the best one could expect of magistrates was damage control. Fortunately, others thought otherwise, as I indicate in my acknowledgments. And, fortunately, they invited me to join the faculty and graduate students they convened every other summer for lively conversations about Augustine's political theology. "Damage control," they persuaded me, required clarification and elaboration. And, if Augustine was as pessimistic about significant political melioration as I was arguing, why did he eagerly counsel leaders of the church and provincial government? Another book.[3]

But my friends and interlocutors, who draw Augustine into studies of contemporary political ethics and political theory as a resource for "hopeful" and "democratic citizenship," raised another question, which I try to answer in this volume. Does a politically pessimistic Augustine offer alternatives worth discussing today, alternatives to the public sphere and to citizenship, as presently defined?

This is occasionally referred to as the "so what" question. As an historian, I found that question disconcerting. To think about relevance and radical alternatives, I needed help. I came across Giorgio Agamben while reading an interpretation of Shakespeare's *Coriolanus*. Its author deployed the prolific and versatile Italian literary and cultural critic, whose take on sovereignty, spectacle, citizenship, alienation, and deactivation was, as I increasingly discovered, similar to Augustine's. Agamben commented favorably, yet only briefly, on Augustine's conventual alternatives to the forms of life or social roles that, both agreed, captivated and captured citizens.[4] Without noting the preeminent position Augustine

---

[3]Peter Iver Kaufman, *Incorrectly Political: Augustine and Thomas More* (Notre Dame: University of Notre Dame Press, 2007); Peter Iver Kaufman, *Augustine's Leaders* (Eugene: Cascade, 2017).
[4]Giorgio Agamben, *Altissima povertà: Regole monastiche e forma di vita* (Milan: Neri Pozza, 2011), 41–42.

reserved for resident aliens or pilgrims passing through (not, as citizens, comfortable in) the terrestrial city, Agamben does consider the refugee or pariah the paradigm for a new historical awareness. He attributes that position to Hannah Arendt who, nonetheless, enters this ensemble for other reasons.[5] For she completed her doctoral dissertation on Augustine's concept of love in 1929, but closed, noting that he had endeavored persistently to set up a compassionate alternative community (*ein Miteinander und Füreinander*) alongside and opposed to conventional societies (*neben und gegen*).[6] Arendt had something of an allergic reaction to the otherworldliness of Augustine's objective. She was bent on contributing to the improvement of political discourse and activity in this world, in the public sphere, until, I argue, her disenchantment with duplicity and intolerance there brought her back to Augustine. Late in her career, she planned to publish an English translation of her dissertation.

Arendt's return to Augustine and her contemplation of alternative poleis constitute the most controversial reading on offer in what follows, yet the introduction of Agamben probably qualifies as a close second. I can only hope that my entry into the history of political theory in the twentieth and twenty-first centuries will be judged as informed and that my interpretations will come across as plausible and, ideally, persuasive. The conceit of this study is simply that, should we draw Arendt and Agamben into conversation with Augustine's political theology—rather than leaving them as passersby—we might find defensible justifications and some fresh applications for the radical alternatives, *neben und gegen*, to what he called "the business of Babylon" and to what passes now as politics as usual in the public realm.

---

[5]Giorgio Agamben, *Mezzi senza fine: Note sulla politica* (Turin: Bollati Boringhieri, 1996), 20–21.
[6]Hannah Arendt, *Der Liebesbegriff bei Augustin: Versuch einer philosophischen Interpretation* (Berlin: Springer, 1929), 86.

ABBREVIATIONS

Augustine's Works

(Abbreviations conform to those in the *Augustinus-Lexikon*. For convenient access to Migne's edition in *Patrologia, series Latina*, see http://www.augustinus.it/latino/index/htm. I have also consulted the more recent critical edition, *Corpus scriptorum ecclesiasticorum Latinorum*).

acad.	De Academicis libri tres.
bapt.	De baptismo libri septem.
c. ep. Man.	Contra epistulam Manichaei quam vocant fundamenti liber unus.
c. ep. Parm.	Contra epistulam Parmeniani libri tres.
c. Faust.	Contra Faustum Manicheum libri triginta tres.
c. Iul.	Contra Iulianum libri sex.
c. Iul. imp.	Contra Iulianum opus imperfectum.
c. litt. Petil.	Contra litteras Petiliani libri tres.
c. Sec.	Contra Secundinum Manicheum liber unus.
cat. rud.	De cathecizandis rudibus liber unus.
civ.	De civitate dei libri viginti duo.
conf.	Confessionum libri tredecim.
Cresc.	Ad Cresconium grammaticum partis Donati libri quattuor.

div. qu.	De diversis quaestionibus octoginta tribus liber unus.
en. Ps.	Enarrationes in Psalmos.
ep.	epistulae.
ep. Io. tr.	In epistulam Iohannis ad Parthos tractatus decem.
exc. urb.	De excidio urbis Romae.
exp. Gal.	Expositio epistulae ad Galatas liber unus.
gest. Pel.	De gestis Pelagii liber unus.
gr. et lib. arb.	De gratia et libero arbitrio liber unus.
Io. ev. tr.	In Iohannis evangelium tractatus CXXIV.
mor.	De moribus ecclesiae catholicae et de moribus Manicheorum libri duo.
op. mon.	De opere monachorum liber unus.
ord.	De ordine libri duo.
pecc. mer.	De peccatorum meritis et remissione et de baptismo parvulorum ad Marcellinum libri tres.
persev.	De dono perseverentiae liber ad Prosperum et Hilarium secundus.
praed. sanct.	De praedestinatione sanctorum liber ad Prosperum et Hilarium secundus.
reg. 2	Regula: Ordo monasterii.
retr.	Retractationum liber duo.
s.	sermones.
Simpl.	Ad Simplicianum libri duo.
sol.	Soliloquiorum libri duo.
spir. et litt.	De spiritu et littera ad Marcellinum liber unus.
trin.	De trinitate liber quindecim.
util. cred.	De utilitate credendi liber unus.
vera rel.	De vera religione liber unus.
virg.	De sancta virginitate liber unus.

1

Augustine and Agamben

To Caecilian

Some historical theologians along with colleagues in political theory and political ethics have been trawling in Augustine's correspondence for resources and endorsements for what one, Charles Mathewes, describes as "hopeful citizenship." These scholars have clear favorites. They nearly always reel in and draw into their arguments for Augustine's critical though progressive approach to political practice Augustine's two long letters to Magistrate Macedonius and a third to Tribune Marcellinus.[1] But one that got away is especially

---

[1] Augustine, ep. 138 (Marcellinus), ep. 153 and ep. 155 (Macedonius). Abbreviations in references to Augustine's correspondence, sermons and treatises conform to those in the *Augustinus-Lexikon*. Access to J. P. Migne's edition of Augustine's works in *Patrologia, series Latina* is convenient—http://www.augustinus.it/latino/index/htm— though I have also consulted the more recent critical edition, *Corpus scriptorium ecclesiasticorum Latinorum*. For "hopeful citizenship," see Charles Mathewes, *A Theology of Public Life* (Cambridge: Cambridge University Press, 2007), 214–18, 242–60 and his *The Republic of Grace: Augustinian Thoughts for Dark Times* (Grand Rapids: Eerdmans, 2010), 68–73, 220–43. Augustine's apparent contributions to an equally hopeful "democratic citizenship" are featured in Eric Gregory, *Politics and the Order of Love: An Augustinian Ethic of Democratic Citizenship* (Chicago: University of Chicago Press, 2008), 107–48 ("Augustinianism as Civic Liberalism") and 350–84 (for Gregory's analysis of a purportedly "Exhausted Politics of Pessimism"). For Augustines who resemble Clinton and Obama Democrats, see Joseph Clair, *Discerning the Good in the Letters and Sermons of Augustine* (Oxford: Oxford University Press, 2016), 80–106 and Michael Lamb, "Between Presumption and Despair: Augustine's Hope for the Commonwealth," *The American Political Science Review* 112 (2018), 1036–49, respectively.

relevant for my purpose in this book, an ambiguous, perplexing letter that a rather demoralized Augustine wrote *about* Marcellinus. It was omitted from the volume of Augustine's "political writings" in the Cambridge University Press series, "Texts in the History of Political Thought." But that letter to Caecilian, an imperial commissioner in Africa—as was Marcellinus—seems a perfect place to crank up a reconsideration of Augustine's interest in citizenship and our assessment of his hopes for late fourth- and early fifth-century Christians who, repudiating obsessions with possessions in this wicked and punishing world, accepted his characterization of their fate as pilgrims.[2]

Augustine wrote after (and about) Marcellinus's execution in late spring, 413. Caecilian's close associate, Marinus, was responsible. He had sailed from Italy to Africa, ostensibly to mop up remnants of what looked to the Roman Senate to have been a consul-elect's conspiracy against the government. Apparently Marcellinus and his brother and fellow statesman Apringius were implicated at the time, although Augustine insisted (and a subsequent exoneration suggests) that they were unfairly accused. He condemned Marinus for having them killed after agreeing to submit the charges against both to judicial review and to await the result of a collateral appeal to the emperor that other African bishops were ferrying to Italy.[3] Augustine was saddened to learn Caecilian and Marinus remained friendly. Their friendship, he wrote, suggested Caecilian had been complicit in the preemptive executions. Augustine prudently—if perhaps disingenuously—dissociated himself from such suspicions; he had heard Caecilian's relations with Marcellinus and Apringius were strained, but he remembered how unnerved Caecilian had been when he brought the bishops news of the terrible crime (*immanis scelus*).[4]

Still, Caecilian's attachment to Marinus obviously irritated Augustine. He appreciated that politics made strange bedfellows, yet

---

[2]Augustine, ep. 151 was omitted from *Augustine: Political Writings*, ed. E. M. Atkins and R. J. Dodaro (Cambridge: Cambridge University Press, 2001). Augustine's comments on the wickedness of this world and the punitive character of ordinary life surface often in his *City of God*. See, for example, Augustine, *civ.* 18.49 (*in hoc saeculo maligno*) and *civ.* 21.14 (*vita ipsa mortalium tota poena sit*).
[3]Augustine, ep. 151.6.
[4]Augustine, ep. 151.10.

he warned Caecilian against amity with Marcellinus's unrepentant executioner, advising that crime was contagious in the corridors of power. Marinus's reprehensible behavior may well have shocked Caecilian as well as Augustine, but the former's ongoing relationship and politic familiarities with Marinus, if conspicuous from then on, would "compel *us*," Augustine wrote, obviously numbering himself among those concerned—"compel us"—to believe otherwise and to believe the worst of his correspondent.[5]

The letter appears to break off abruptly. The last surviving lines berate Caecilian for being reluctant to proceed from the catechumenate to baptism. Did the imperial commissioner believe he could not simultaneously be a good Christian and a proficient politician?[6] Augustine occasionally encountered concerns of that sort and warily argued that faith and civic piety were not incompatible.[7] Yet the letter to Caecilian contains, in addition to what verged on political pandering, questions and conditional clauses (*si verum quaeris audire*) indicating that Augustine doubted the commissioner's probity and candor. He apparently thought Caecilian had given an inadequate account of his ignorance and innocence. He pressed the commissioner to let on where he had been during Marcellinus's execution. If absent, how did he hear of it, and what did he say to Marinus when he learned of the executioner's deceit and rush to misjudgment?[8] The letter's tone is respectful, to a point. But for a stretch, it becomes an inquisition, as if Marinus's intrigues and Marcellinus's murder jolted Augustine and stirred him to recall the loathing of political necessities, niceties, and frauds that moved him years before to repudiate his own political ambitions. Marinus's ruthlessness, its fatal consequences, and Caecilian's questionable conduct prompted Augustine to leave Carthage quite soon after Marcellinus's and Apringius's deaths to avoid the compliance and courtesies expected of the province's bishops, despite the outrages committed by political officials.[9]

---

[5] Augustine, ep. 151.7: *Sed plane fateor, si etiam posthac in ea familiaritate estis in qua antea fuistis, pace tua sit liber dolor, multum nos quod nolebamus compellitis credere.*
[6] Augustine, ep. 151.14: *Unum est autem . . . quod in te molestissime fero.*
[7] Augustine, ep. 138.12-13 and ep. 189.5-6.
[8] Augustine, ep. 151.12 and 14.
[9] Augustine, ep. 151.3: *Cum tantum malum nullo pectoris robore potuissem tolerare, discessi.*

Of course, he could hardly have avoided contact and courtesies altogether. African bishops needed to remain on good terms with government officials whose support for Catholic Christianity was critical. Before he had been apprehended and executed, Marcellinus reinstated the penalties intended to force Donatist dissidents to conform and reconcile; enforcement of the edicts depended on the cooperation of local and provincial authorities. The Donatists, rivals for African Christians' loyalties, were thought to have endorsed their most militant members' efforts to intimidate Catholic Christian prelates, so, if Augustine is to be trusted, the government was all that stood between sectarian extremists and their victims among his colleagues.[10] Moreover—and quite apart from the schism that had divided North African Christianity for a century—all bishops were obliged to cultivate political officials to ensure their interventions on behalf of parishioners petitioning for relief or privilege were taken seriously. So, although he probed for scraps of the story that would either exonerate or incriminate Caecilian, Augustine was generally diplomatic. He discreetly complained that envy and deceit tended to capsize good reputations and even to end the lives of creditable public servants. But his compendious *City of God*, which he started composing a few years earlier, railed against political treachery and the lust for domination that fueled it. We shall attend to his comments on the latter in the next chapter, yet what he seems to have alluded to as he confronted Caecilian and to have lamented in his *City* looks comparable to what Giorgio Agamben characterizes as a state of exception, in which sovereign powers perpetuate anxieties that justify suspending due process.[11]

What follows in this chapter and at the start of the next docks Agamben's insights about sovereignty and citizenship alongside Augustine's remarks about civic piety, pilgrimage, and a pervasive, contagious concupiscence—the inordinate, insatiable desire to acquire wealth, glory, and territory that made for political malpractice. The result of this juxtaposition ought to prompt

---

[10]See, for example, Augustine, ep. 76.2, ep. 88.1, ep. 93.2-4, ep. 105.3, and ep. 185.21-23; Augustine, *c. ep. Parm.* 2.9,19; and Augustine, *Cresc.* 3.42.46-47 and 4.50,60.
[11]Compare Augustine ep. 151.4 and Augustine, *civ.* 9.14 with Giorgio Agamben, *Stato di eccezione* (Turin: Bollati Boringhieri, 2003), 34–35, 55–56.

greater appreciation for the trajectory, comprehensiveness, and fervor of Augustine's criticisms of late antique political culture. The current chapter also sifts several of his alternatives to enthusiastic (or lunatic) participation in the pageants of public life, central to which was a passionate commendation of compassion and the proposition—which will seem, at first, to undermine that commendation—that pilgrims passing through this world to a celestial city temperamentally disengage from political and commercial life, that they harbor different hopes from those of hopeful citizens. For Augustine and Agamben, who made refugees the heralds of his "new politics," the concepts of "citizen" and "citizenship" acted as drugs that kept (and still keep) subjects from seeing clearly their callings (Augustine) and potentials (Agamben).[12]

Augustine: Politically prominent friends

Marcellinus's fate, much as the fate of fourth-century Christian emperors whose faith failed to preserve them from misfortune, probably called to Augustine's mind the instructions he had written for colleagues who prepared Christians for baptism. He told them to advise catechumens that their faith promised no advancement in this world. Christianity offered no guarantee against inclement weather, lost revenue, or untimely death. Indeed, catechumens must learn that only when worldly advantage was acknowledged as an impediment to humility—and as precarious—could the power of God's love inspire their commitments to love God in return and pay God's love forward by loving others.[13] Cathechumens' and parishioners' expectations to the contrary made Augustine cringe. Evil was everywhere, inescapable (*abundant mala*). Most humans were selfish; their cupidity and indiscipline made this world unstable. Marinus's purge was but one of the many flagrant miscarriages of justice in Roman history. Augustine thought his

---

[12] Augustine, *civ.* 18.54 and Giorgio Agamben, *L'uso dei corpi* (Vicenza: Neri Pozza, 2014), 346–47.
[13] Augustine, *cat. rud.* 16.24. Also, in this connection, see Salvino Biolo, "L'amore umano come ponte sull'eterno secondo S. Agostino," in *L'umanesimo di Sant'Agostino*, ed. Matteo Fabris (Bari: Università degli studi di Bari, 1986), 70–72.

contemporary Orosius was mistaken to think that persecutions of Christianity would pass. Statesmen who possessed Marcellinus's virtue and tact were rare. Most politically prominent provincial officials, even if tolerant of their emperors' faith and cordial to its prelatical overseers, could merely minimize the effects of greed and malevolence. It's true that damage control was part of God's management strategy. Yet, despite edicts favorable to Christianity issued by emperors Constantine and Theodosius, creation as a whole was beyond recall. Enough might be done, however, to extend God's love to some.[14]

Felices spe: only hope for celestial peace beyond the grave brought lasting happiness to Christian magistrates, even Christian emperors. They may have taken pleasure subduing rebellions, planning public works, and formulating legislation aimed at improving citizens' status and morale, yet Augustine was skeptical about their efforts to enlist bishops in schemes supposedly designed to create or preserve social harmony. Emperor Constantine—after having tolerated, then indulged, Christianity—promised prelates that they would be free from temporal duties to attend exclusively to their sacramental and spiritual work. But he seems to have subsequently changed his mind and policy. Likely to streamline the administration of justice, Constantine directed bishops to preside over diocesan courts, exposing them to a battery of complaints—not only complaints they heard in their chambers or "audiences" but also protests questioning their fairness in the aftermath of arbitrations. Perhaps the emperor shared such suspicions, because he soon adjusted the jurisdiction of the churches' courts, stipulating restrictions that could signal he had been disabused of the idea that bishops were better than other bureaucrats at resisting affluent litigants' improper influence.[15]

---

[14]Augustine, s. 80.8. For Augustine and Orosius's optimism, see Domenico Marafioti, "Comme leggere il *De civitate Dei*," *Augustinianum* 53 (2013), 463–64.

[15]H. A. Drake, *Constantine and the Bishops: The Politics of Intolerance* (Baltimore: Johns Hopkins University Press, 2002), 323–29, 344–46. Also see John Lamoreaux, "Episcopal Courts in Late Antiquity," *Journal of Early Christian Studies* 3 (995), 148–50 and Kevin Uhalde, *Expectations of Justice in the Age of Augustine* (Philadelphia: University of Pennsylvania Press, 2007), 52–53, 135–37. Claims that Augustine became interested in expanding the jurisdiction of the church's courts were registered by Kauko Raikas, "*Audientia Episcopalis*: Problematik zwischen Staat und Kirche

North Africa's bishops, for their part, seem to have accepted that, as beneficiaries of the empire's relative peace, they were obliged to cooperate in keeping it. But Augustine disliked his court work. He explained that the government's outsourcing arbitration in uncivil disputes placed him in a difficult position. Those parishioners who litigated and lost were often unwilling to turn a page when their bishops ceased being umpires and again became pastors. The disappointed regularly refused to submit to pastoral guidance.[16] Late in his career, Augustine nominated a successor and assigned diocesan court duties to him. But, by then, other civic responsibilities had fallen to bishops in Africa as the increasing financial burdens of public service discouraged the municipal elites from participation in government; bishops' participation in what Augustine came to call "the business of Babylon" grew greater than he would have wanted.[17]

Augustine was thus suggesting that greater political prominence complicated bishops' pastoral work, specifically, their reliance on less litigious ways to discipline their parishioners. Yet he admitted that sacraments and sermons left too many Catholic Christians committed or "cured" only to a point. Not yet truly grateful for God's grace and unfamiliar with, or indifferent to, their faith's implications for behavior, they could imperil coreligionists.[18] The more militant dissident Donatist Christians were a prime example; they assaulted Catholic Christian prelates, intimidated the Catholic Christian laity, and—Augustine's reports of their stunning and sometimes suicidal initiatives alleged—edged the African provinces to the brink of uncivil war. Catholic Christianity's bishops figured that they had no alternative, save to mobilize their prominent political friends, and that they were much better positioned to do so, if they, too, were involved in governance, in that business of

---

bei Augustin," *Augustinianum* 37 (1997), 476–77 as well as by Claude Lepelley, "Liberté, colonat, et esclavage d'après la lettre 24*: La jurisdiction épiscopale *de liberali causa*," in *Les lettres de saint Augustin découvertes par Joannes Divjak*, ed. Lepelley (Paris: Études augustiniennes, 1983), 340–42. For an alternative reading of the evidence, see my, "Augustine, Macedonius, and the Courts," *Augustinian Studies* 34 (2003), 67–81.

[16] Augustine, *en Ps.* 86.6.
[17] Augustine, ep. 213.5. Also see Augustine, *op. mon.* 37.
[18] Augustine, s. 131.6.

Babylon. So, without completely suppressing his opinion that such involvement too often poisoned parish relations, Augustine bowed to the inevitable.[19]

He fashioned claims that were likely appeal to public officials. He compared Catholic Christians to the myriad stars in the heavens and Donatists to strays, although, in the late 380s, when Augustine returned from Italy to Numidia, there—and likely in proconsular Africa as well—Donatists outnumbered Catholics.[20] And the former, for nearly a century, as Joseph Ratzinger explains, had come to consider antipathy to government "essential" and "existential." Donatists insisted that cooperation with prominent provincial authorities was inappropriate; Augustine viewed it as tactical.[21]

Catholic Christianity's highly placed friends in local and provincial government increased its chances of ending the schism to its bishops' advantage. But Christians of all stripes were well served by having politically prominent friends who might offer protection from unruly pagans. Paganism was more than a nuisance in fifth-century North Africa. Marianne Kah's study proposes that the edicts from the courts of emperors Theodosius and Honorius prohibiting public pagan displays opened rather than foreclosed debates. Incidents in the cities of Sufes (Byzacena) and Calama (Numidia, only seventy or so kilometers from Hippo Regius and Augustine) proved that debates could turn violent, dynamite whatever *d'etente* prevailed between Christians and pagans, and cost the former their properties, churches, and lives. So, if pilgrims to the celestial city were to stay safe in their terrestrial cities, their bishops would be well advised to court the provincial officials who had the wherewithal, if not always the will, to bridle reckless pagans, punish disorderly Donatists, and overawe yet-to-be-effectively-disciplined Catholics.[22]

---

[19]For example, see Augustine, ep. 86.1, ep. 100.1-2, ep. 133.1-3, ep. 185.46-47, and ep. 204.6-9.
[20]Augustine, ep. 93.28-30.
[21]Joseph Ratzinger, *Volk und Haus Gottes in Augustins Lehre von der Kirche* (Munich: Zink, 1954), 310–11: *eine Wesenfrage des christlichen Seins*.
[22]Marianne Kah, *"Die Welt der Römer mit der Seele suchend": Die Religiosität des Prudentius im Spannungsfeld zwischen "Pietas Christiana" und "Pietas Romana"* (Bonn: Borengässer, 1989), 127–28. For Calama, see Kaufman, "Patience and/or Politics: Augustine and the Crisis of Calama," VC 57 (2003), 22–35 and for Sufes, see Julio César Magalhães de Oliveira, "*Ut majores pagani non sint*! Pouvoir,

Safety was significant, of course, but bishops' politically influential friends could do nothing of consequence about the predicament largely responsible for disconcertingly pervasive dangers, specifically, humanity's servitude to envy and ambition, which made political culture a rather wretched affair. Augustine's *City of God* itemized some consolations (*solacia*). Healthy bodies—intricate networks of arteries and veins—attested the creator's craftsmanship. Humans were creative and procreative. Conspicuous improvements in health care and navigation were epic. Absent from Augustine's inventory of consolations, however, was hope for meaningful political melioration.[23]

Marinus—and, presumably, Caecilian, to whom Augustine wrote about the executions of Marcellinus and Apringius—were no exceptions to the rule that rule was cruel. Augustine knew too much about political history to suggest that Marinus's cruelty and deceit were unparalleled. Still, Marinus, Caecilian, and most of their colleagues in government generally attended to the needs of Catholic Christian churches during Augustine's pontificate. Donatists' participation in an insurgency in the late 390s almost certainly motivated provincial officials to enforce Emperor Honorius's edicts against them, particularly after the decrees acquired what Pietro Romanelli calls "new vitality" by the murder of Stilicho, who had suppressed that rebellion.[24]

African Catholic bishops again needed their prominent political friends' protection, and the imperial government responded by sending Tribune Marcellinus from Italy. Augustine came to Carthage to meet him, apparently after the tribune called the

---

iconoclasme, et action populaire à Carthage au début du Vᵉ siècle," *Antiquité tardive* 14 (2006), 246–62.

[23] Augustine, *civ.* 22.24.

[24] See Pietro Romanelli, *Storia delle province romane dell'Africa* (Rome: Bretschneider, 1959), 625–29. For the insurrection, consult W. H. C. Frend, *The Donatist Church: A Movement of Protest in Roman North Africa* (Oxford: Clarendon, 1985), 224–26. Brent D. Shaw, *Sacred Violence: African Christians and Sectarian Hatred in the Age of Augustine* (Cambridge: Cambridge University Press, 2011), 48–50, doubts the evidence for the seriousness of the insurgency and the extent of the Donatist involvement. Augustine, *c. litt. Pet.* 1.24, 26 perhaps invents—but certainly stresses—the conspiracy between Donatist bishop Optatus of Thamugadi and the rebels' leader, Gildo. Might we assume, though, that any level of dissident collaboration—real or just reputed—would have worried officials?

factions to a council, but before the African prelates assembled. Catholic Christian bishops' overtures and fines assigned by the government had, to that point, failed to draw the Donatists into African churches in communion with those elsewhere in the empire. The council convened in 411, and the purportedly verbatim account shows that, at the third and final session, Augustine was by far the most resourceful and effective polemicist. He fired salvo after salvo, charging proto-Donatists with secession early in the fourth century and their descendants in the fifth with obstinacy for refusing to reconcile. He embroidered his presentation with a series of succinct scriptural expositions correcting sectarian misinterpretations of sacred texts and misrepresentations of the history of the schism. Augustine documented Donatist overtures (and failures) to win political backing, thereby invalidating their complaints that Catholic Christians in the African provinces initially and inappropriately invited Rome to referee an ecclesiastical quarrel. He thus undermined sectarian opposition to political intervention. For his part, Marcellinus renewed and set about to enforce the penalties suspended to give Donatists some hope that conferring might lead to a permanent improvement in their position.[25]

But Augustine understood that penalties would only be successful to a point. Depriving the Donatists of their basilicas and prelates might get dissident laity into Catholic Christianity's churches, yet coercion was unlikely to win over hearts and minds. The entire apparatus of earthly judgment—fines, confiscations, and exile— would be less effective than the resources available to the Catholic bishops who were known for having censured relentlessly (*arguimus, increpimus, detestamur*), but who also featured the forgiveness, compassion, and reconciliation on offer in their congregations.[26] Statesmen could only accomplish so much. Augustine recalled that King Nebuchadnezzar had promoted Shadrach, Meschach, and Abednego to posts in Babylon; as their sovereign's servants, the

---

[25] For an example of the Donatists' strategy, see *Actes de la Conférence de Carthage en 411*, vol. 3, ed. Serge Lancel (Paris: Cerf, 1975), 1138–40. The third volume reports Augustine's various rebuttals on most pages. Also see Émilien Lamirande, "La Conférence de Carthage (411) et les réactions de Saint Augustin: Un procès singulier fatal aux Donatistes," *Studia Canonica* 32 (1998), 415–40.
[26] Augustine, ep. 153.21.

three Jews set a biblical precedent for the Christian magistrates in late antiquity, people of the celestial Jerusalem who, although only pilgrims in this world, had been selected to give or preserve order to the business of Babylon. They ought not to prolong their service, Augustine implied, and they must never seem to be at home in what James Wetzel, channeling him, describes as a "ragingly imperfect" world which, Augustine observed, was perpetually perishing (*transitura*). Christian magistrates' spiritual guides were not to discourage them. The faithful were to serve their sovereigns in the company of, yet never comfortable with, other public servants who were at ease, despite the imperfection—at ease, at home, and in authority.[27]

The world was imperfect, in part, because political cultures, in Augustine's view, could never generate or become effective remedies for ambition and envy. The reason seemed simple: politics ran on ambition and envy. Christians serving local, provincial, and imperial governments could not change that, even if they exhibited the humility of Emperor Theodosius or the goodwill of Marcellinus. Nearing the conclusion of his *City of God*, Augustine packed observations into a cramped section, a hive of accusations that—along with his comments on the lust for domination pervasive among politicians, which we shall explore more fully in the next chapter—demonstrate just how intractable the problems confronting political leaders were: humans tirelessly probe for fresh ways to victimize each other. Societies lurched from brutality or barbarism to humiliation and, occasionally, civilization before cruelty resurfaced, to tragic effect. Political leaders' feverish efforts to forestall or limit damage (if subjects were lucky) or to harass and molest constituents (if they were not) alternated with indolence.[28]

Plausibly, there was some comfort for pilgrims, knowing that such a world was perishing as well as imperfect. It would end; they would go on. How and when it would end, however, was unknowable; the apostles had not been told, so their clerical descendants in the African churches could hardly expect privileged information. They were wise to steer clear of questions they were ill-equipped to

---

[27] Augustine, *en. Ps.* 61.8, citing Dan. 3:30; James Wetzel, "A Tangle of Two Cities," *Augustinian Studies* 43 (2012), 12.
[28] Augustine, *civ.* 22.22.

answer, but Augustine appreciated that the uncertainty remained problematic for Christian bishops as long as parishioners, watching the wicked prosper and the righteous suffer, inquired why a reversal had been delayed and when it might be expected. How were prelates to respond satisfactorily? They could only shore up faith *that* God's purposes would be realized without saying *how* or *when*.[29] They could say, in the interim, that the church's politically prominent friends and prelates would undertake discipline and damage control, criminalizing wickedness and making the dreadful somewhat less dreaded. Augustine allowed that Christian magistrates, to some extent, conforming to this world's customs and expectations (*aliquantulum congruamus*), might use their positions to persuade the convoys of petitioners and litigants who solicited their favor not to pursue personal advantage to the exclusion of all else. Compassion could be catching, moreover; magistrates might inspire mercy in others.[30] Yet Augustine was quick to point out that compassion and coercion or correction were compatible. On occasion, the duty to love would require Christian magistrates to prosecute conduct that disrupted the business of Babylon he criticized.[31] All to the good, if tough love inspired some love—if only a skimpy sum. If Augustine were right, then astute, penitent offenders would come to see how and why compassion heals by paying forward God's love for creation in neighbor-love. Censure, accompanied or followed by instruction, can, he believed, make offenders remorseful. And remorse can lead to rehabilitation. Rehabilitation, of course, was not redemption. Only God could move the sinful—from within—to embrace faith, Augustine often explained, but Christian statesmen and their churches' politically prominent friends (as well as their churches) had parts to play in assisting miscreants to renounce their inordinate desires to acquire and their practices, which had come to seem normal—and normative—in this wicked world, but which jeopardized practitioners' standing in the next.[32]

---

[29] Augustine, *c. Faust.* 22.78 (*distributio judicantis et miserentis*); Augustine, s. 27.6-7.
[30] Augustine, *c. ep. Parm.* 3.2.13 (*In qua tanto est efficacior emendatio pravitatis, quanto diligentior conservatio caritatis*) is the closest Augustine came to making this link. For magistrates and litigants, Augustine, ep. 95.2.
[31] Augustine, ep. 105.13 and 153.19.
[32] Augustine, *civ.* 18.49.

With a nod to Nietzsche, not to Augustine, Giorgio Agamben similarly suggests that a proper perspective on what passes as normal or normative requires distance and disconnection from the ordinary (*una sconnessione*; *una sfasatura*; *discronia*). Agamben refers to Augustine only rarely. He identifies what he calls an authentic experience of the inauthenticity of political and commercial regimes—an experience we soon try to fathom—with late antique Gnosticism's effort to break cosmic laws and overcome the world's estrangement from God.[33] But in one of his most revealing intersections with Augustine, Agamben finds the bishop's alternative to the normal and normative, an alternative "form of life," appealing—even inspiring.[34] Perhaps, had he treated himself to a steadier diet of Augustine, Agamben might have grown fond of the ardor and frequency with which he urged the faithful to turn away from Babylon and, as pilgrims, to adopt a refugee's or pariah's perspective on their time in time. Augustine tried to reconcile pilgrims to their estrangement from this wicked world, to decathect or emotionally disengage when pressed into public service, to flee from seductions associated with temporal advantages, and to develop an altogether different kind of hope, faith, and affection from those of this world's sovereign powers.[35]

Augustine's pilgrims

Recommendations that reflect Augustine's faith in—and his hopes and affection for—communities of refugees or pilgrims came later and often in his sermons but were foreshadowed in remarks about his experiences and experiments with what Peter Brown calls "commune[s] of like-minded souls."[36] As a young scholar and ambitious orator-in-training, Augustine was drawn to conversations

---

[33] For example, see Agamben, *Nudità* (Rome: Nottetemp, 2009), 19–20; Agamben, *Infanzia e storia: Distruzione dell'esperienza e origine della storia* (Turin: Einaudi, 2001), 106–7.
[34] Agamben, *Altissima povertà*, 42–43.
[35] Augustine, *en. Ps.* 64.2 and 136.1; Augustine, *civ.* 18.54.
[36] Peter Brown, *Through the Eye of a Needle: Wealth, the Fall of Rome, and the Making of Christianity in the West, 350–550 AD* (Princeton: Princeton University Press, 2012), 161–62.

with Manichees, devotees of the third-century Persian prophet Mani. Their elite or specialists addressed many of the issues about which he was curious. But he became friendlier with their admirers or auditors and, it seems, persuaded a few of his other companions to join their cohort in Carthage, if not also—for a time—in Italy. Indeed, after he grew disenchanted with the sect's esoteric cosmology and counsels, he remained involved with the sect for the camaraderie, he said; Manichaean doctrine disappointed, and the leadership seemed ignorant and arrogant as well as immoral to him, if we may trust what he wrote after breaking with them altogether, but he confided that he had feared losing his friends in the sect, if he aired any complaints.[37] And, on the verge of leaving or just after he disengaged, he looked to assemble some of those friends who happened to be with him in Milan to form a commune in 385. They would pool their resources to live and study apart from the crowds, but the wives of several prospects objected, and the scheme was scuttled.[38] The following year, Augustine tried again. He collected a few friends at a villa at Cassiciacum, thirty miles from Milan. They lived communally, talked and studied for a few months, and they left enough evidence of their fellowship to permit us some generalizations.[39]

Licentius, the son of Augustine's longtime friend and patron Romanianus, joined his father at Cassiciacum and composed a tribute to the affections developed there (*hic, hic regnet amicitia*). If Licentius is to be believed, the company at Cassiciacum was thrilled to be far from the crowds in the city frantically chasing after material advantage. Augustine was the impresario; Cassiciacum colleagues would have read less—and less profitably—Licentius said, had Augustine not motivated them. But Licentius also emphasized that the goodwill binding the commune was so robust that Hannibal who long ago had breathtakingly cut through the nearby Alps to

---

[37] Augustine, *conf.* 3.6.10–3.7.12; 4.8,13; and 5.10,18. Also see Augustine, *util. cred.* 14.31 and Jason David BeDuhn, *Augustine's Manichaean Dilemma: Conversion and Apostasy, 373–388 C.E.* (Philadelphia: University of Pennsylvania Press, 2009), 187.
[38] Augustine, *conf.* 6.14,24.
[39] Dennis Trout, "Augustine at Cassiciacum: *Otium Honestam* and the Social Dimensions of Conversion," *VC* 42 (1988), 132–46; Danuta Shanzer, "*Arcanum Varronis iter*: Licentius's Verse Epistle to Augustine," *Revue d'Études Augustiniennes* 37 (1991), 124–26.

bedevil Italy (*Alpes fregit*) could never have fractured the friendships at the villa.⁴⁰

Augustine had doubts. The *Soliloquies* he composed at Cassiciacum or soon after his return to Milan confided that the prospect of losing friends terribly distressed him (*facit animo aegritudinem*). And he was brutally frank about his take on the limits of Licentius's enthusiasm. Despite his effusive praise for friendship and study, Licentius seemed to Augustine to be flirting with distractions, to be susceptible to the snares set by ordinary affairs (*vincula . . . hujus mundi*) trapping and holding him close to the kind of concerns citizens of the terrestrial city were unable to sidestep. Augustine lectured Licentius about the need to disavow this world's counterfeit joys and to commit to contemplation, conversation, and friendship.⁴¹ And, not long after he returned to Africa, Augustine enjoined another of his Cassiciacum colleagues, Nebridius, to avoid affairs that preoccupied others. Crowds and the rewards one earned by catering to them were obstacles to experiencing a sturdier, substantial happiness (*solidum gaudium*) that would only be possible after a withdrawal and self-imposed exile of sorts (*magna secessione a tumultu*).⁴²

Sermons Augustine subsequently and sometimes peevishly preached inventoried dangers associated with devotion to the crowds' amusements and to the business of Babylon. Desires for solvency were irresistible, Augustine admitted, yet he harped on the disorientation occasioned by citizens' *idée fixe*, by their intense concentration on material and political advantages. He said they were "at sea." But he also realized that the faithful could not hide in a sect sealed off from the cares afflicting their neighbors. Devout Christians would always be happier in port (*feliciores in portu quam in pelago*). But their ports or communities ought to have openings, an access to the world around them, if only to welcome any who found their harbors attractive.⁴³ Augustine imagined that studious colleagues might be drawn away from Babylon's "snares" and

---

⁴⁰Augustine, ep. 26.3.
⁴¹Augustine, *sol.* 1.9.16; Augustine, ep. 26.2 and ep. 27.6.
⁴²Augustine, ep. 10.2.
⁴³Augustine, *en. Ps.* 99.9-11. Also see Tarsicius Jan van Bavel, *La communauté selon Augustin: Une grâce pour notre temps* (Brussels: Lessius, 2000), 105-7.

close to each other once they became nauseated by their neighbors' fascination with the fashionable and love for luxury. Some only seemed at home in the world. They went through the motions, as it were, but the gusto was missing. Their own scandalous behavior upset them. Augustine thought he could discern as much along with enough evidence of their civility, which, in the proper port, could grow into affection for learning and for others engaged in study.[44]

After he left Italy for Africa, Augustine set up a commune of sorts on his family's estate in Thagaste. The fellowship there was held together by a common resolve rather than by vows or rules. But one could say that, in Augustine's scheme, compassion was the rule, distinguishing the Thagaste community from the commercial and political traffic he associated with the business of Babylon, which rewarded persons selling, swindling, or dominating—rather than loving—others.[45] When he accepted clerical responsibilities, he took much the same line. He instructed catechists to raise the horizon of neophytes' expectations, that is, to substitute hopes for a celestial reward for their longing to achieve respectability, influence, and temporal advantages.[46] He let instructors add inflection, trusting they would be the appropriate judges of neophytes' receptivity. The attachments of some to the faith were frivolous. They and others would simply ignore religious precepts they considered intrusive. There was much chaff in the church, Augustine noticed after passing time as priest and bishop, though undoubtedly before as well—and not just chaff but wolves among the clergy preying on the sheep.[47] But, for all that, Augustine trusted that catechists and their fellow pilgrims in the church could assist the elect to avoid temptations and bad influences and complete what Sarah Stewart-Kroeker calls the faithful sojourners' "formative journey."[48]

So the church was *permixta*, a collection of the saintly and the sinful—and a challenge. Augustine seems to have had no qualms about conveying principles in his subsequent pastoral works,

---

[44] Augustine, *Acad.* 2.2.6.
[45] Augustine, *vera rel.* 35.65. Serge Lancel, *Saint Augustin* (Paris: Fayard, 1999), 319 refers to the Thagaste community as "quasi monastic."
[46] Augustine, *cat. rud.* 16.24 and 19.31.
[47] Augustine, *bapt.* 6.1: *lupi . . . qui videtur quidem intus esse*.
[48] Sarah Stewart-Kroeker, *Pilgrimage as Moral and Aesthetic Formation in Augustine's Thought* (Oxford: Oxford University Press, 2017), 163–64.

principles that guided his friends at Cassiciacum and Thagaste, although those "retreats" were "notably unchurched," as Peter Brown reminds us.[49] They were what he probably hoped the congregations under his supervision could become—safe harbors or ports for friends who were recuperating from the dis-ease that self-love and competition for fame and funds perpetuated. Convalescents shared a love for God and, in Augustine's alternative conventual communities, shared a love for learning. Certainly in the churches and almost certainly in the communities at Cassiciacum, Thagaste, and, later, Hippo, Augustine expected that their love for God would get pilgrims, for God's sake, to encourage the love for God they discerned in their friends' love for them.[50] His sermons implored parishioners to forego excuses for failing to see God's love at work in sojourners' affections and for failing to pay God's love forward.[51] But, he conceded, outside those safe harbors the bustling late Roman world was something of a zero-sum game; egregiously uncharitable citizens, he said, rejoiced in their gains, notwithstanding any neighbor's corresponding losses. But competition was a common cultural practice, which, we now know, Augustine thought indelibly marked by envy and ambition. So when Augustine preached to parishioners about spaces (or oases, ports, and harbors) where pilgrims might enrich each other—without losses to any—he conceivably reminisced about his countercultural experiments.[52]

Nonsense? Perhaps, for we cannot say with certainty what was on his mind as he pitched charity to parishioners. But his hymn-like homilies exalting mutually beneficial affections that structured desires, lifted spirits above surging lusts, sustained solidarity, and undermined tyranny masquerading as civic piety line up compatibly with his fond remarks about Cassiciacum and Thagaste.[53]

---

[49]Peter Brown, *Augustine of Hippo* (Berkeley: University of California, 2000), 171. Also see George Lawless, *Augustine of Hippo and His Monastic Rule* (Oxford: Clarendon, 1990), 51–53 and Robin Lane Fox, *Augustine: Conversions to Confessions* (New York: Basic Books, 2015), 381–82.
[50]Augustine, *c. Faust.* 22.78: *Propter Deum enim amat amicum, qui Dei amorem amat in amico.*
[51]Augustine, s. 32.23: *non nos excusemus.*
[52]Augustine, s. 32.21: *justitiam ambo complectimini, et ambo dilatimini.*
[53]In this connection, see, for example, Augustine, *trin.* 8.4-10 and Augustine, s. 45.6-8 and s. 56.16.

Yet those two communities and, apparently, the conventual communities he anchored off his churches in Hippo were devoted to learned conversation in ways that congregations were not. The conversations—imagined or reconstructed—were packed into some of Augustine's early texts and reveal as much. His dialogue with Adeodatus in his *De magistro*, the exchanges in his *Contra academicos*, and the give-and-take with Evodius in his *De libero arbitrio* also reveal conferees' contempt for *negotium*. And, Augustine remembered, those conversations inspired (and disclosed) conferees' love for the love of God they perceived in each other.[54] Interlocutors looked to Augustine for leadership and inspiration; participants, Phillip Carey infers from surviving evidence, were uninterested in "tandem mystical experience[s]" or "simultaneous trance[s]."[55] Conversations were undertaken as mutually edifying alternatives to the eulogies, histrionics, invectives, and seemingly interminable—arguably aimless—philosophical disputes that Augustine and his companions thought off-putting. Only the foolish would think such arguments fruitful and mistake talk touting civic virtues for genuine virtue.[56]

No "amen" has been pronounced over conjectures about the effects of invasions on civic piety in Thrace in the late fourth century and in Italy in the early fifth. But we know that Africa, relatively safe and prosperous at the time, became a refuge. And we know that many of the exiles of senatorial rank, clutching tenaciously what was left of their possessions as they disembarked, sickened Augustine, who was upset as well with a number of his neighbors, inhospitable hosts along the coast who hoarded what they had. Maybe his indignation grew as he remembered the disinterested benevolence at Cassiciacum and Thagaste—as well as at the monastic communities he promoted in Hippo.[57] He appreciated that exile was an ordeal. He told one émigré whom he admired,

---

[54]Augustine, *ord.* 2.9.27.
[55]Phillip Cary, *Outward Signs: The Powerlessness of External Things in Augustine's Thought* (Oxford: Oxford University Press, 2004), 184–85.
[56]Augustine, *Acad.* 3.17, 37.
[57]For refugees, see *Gesta collationis carthaginiensis* 1.149. For the importance of benevolence, consult Gerhard Krieger, "Selig wer Dich liebt und den Freund in Dir: Augustinus und Freundschaft," in *Unruhig ist under Herz: Interpretationen zu Augustins "Confessiones,"* ed. Michael Fiedrowicz (Trier: Paulinus, 2004), 55–56.

the widow Proba, that refugees were justified in husbanding their resources. Excess, however, was evil, he said; the goal ought to be to live as a person of integrity, for whom it was inappropriate to want more than would be sufficient to preserve self-worth. Refugees in diaspora would find friends, he continued, if they extended friendship liberally. And before leaving the topic he mused that it was most gratifying to befriend those close at hand who returned one's love, creating a compassionate company and some comfort for all.[58]

Pelagians were among the refugees from Italy. If they believed their leading theorists, they would assume they were distinguished from other Christians by the confidence they could experience that comfort without repeated divine assistance. Augustine thought such confidence unfortunate and irreverent. He emphasized to Proba, while discussing the heart's "ascent" in prayer, that preparation for prayer, much as compassion, was God's gift. Other loves were clotted with self-interest. A righteousness that overcame *amor sui* and led to the comfort that the faithful experienced in each other's company was reachable only because God reached out first, granting faith and love, and continued reaching out to sustain both. From 410, and for the next twenty years, Augustine's principal pastoral and polemical challenge was to make that point, defending divine sovereignty and saving Christians from the consequences of self-assertion.[59] Yet Johannes Brachtendorf, taking the *Confessions* as an accurate account of Augustine's sentiments in the late fourth century, thinks a "decentering of the self"—and an openness to radical contingency—set him against self-righteousness even before he was a committed Christian and long before he was locked in combat with Pelagians.[60]

There is some risk in adopting Brachtendorf's view, inasmuch as the text of the *Confessions* may say more about the confessor in the late 390s than about his subject (and himself) in the 370s and 380s. But, if we may trust the narrative's passages about a friend's

---

[58] Augustine, ep. 130.12-13, quoting 1 Tim. 6:6-10.
[59] For example, Augustine, *spir. et litt.* 36.65. For advice to Proba on prayer, see Augustine, ep. 130.17.
[60] Johannes Brachtendorf, "Damit sie weinen lernen im Tal der Tränen: Augustinus und die christliche Rehabilitation der Affekte," in *Unruhig ist unser Herz*, 137.

death—and leave for a moment the issue of arrogance—we have located Augustine's first serious effort to assess the importance of companionship. For a small raft of friends found him mired in mourning and self-pity in the early 370s. They were intent on consoling him and kept constant watch over him. He, in turn, was impressed by their affection but also, he said, by the quality of their conversations. They often disagreed—though never acrimoniously. They displayed tremendous affection for each other and for him. Petty jealousies never surfaced. Augustine attributed his recovery from grief to their company and compassion.[61]

His account of the episode suggests to Luigi Franco Pizzolato that his "decentering" was partial or temporary, that self-importance seeps into the narrative of his grief and consolation. That the friends who had consoled him were probably Manichees matters less to Pizzolato than the narrative's egocentricity. Only later, when the shared dedication to pay God's love for creation forward characterized communities Augustine influenced, did what Pizzolato depicts as the optimal interpenetration of friendship and selfless love (*interazione ed una compenetrazione*) become—for Augustine—a spur to compassion. The lessons, then, were learned gradually: (1) attributing the success of those communities to God's love and (2) accepting the impossibility of human nature ever overcoming self-indulgence without God's help were critical to cultivating the humility that became a contributing cause of that success.[62] The communities themselves reinforced the notion that members were sojourners, pilgrims learning love in what Sarah Stewart-Kroeker describes as "neighbor-relations" that become critical to each participant's "moral-aesthetic formation."[63]

It began suddenly with an infusion of God's love, but moral formation was gradual, and along the way, pilgrims learned to pardon. Augustine increasingly teased from the sacred texts' parables the imperative to forgive. Whereas his polemical treatises demonstrate undeniable intransigence, his pastoral work, a number of his letters and many sermons, urged others to give up

---

[61] Augustine, *conf.* 4.8,13; also see Augustine, *cat. rud.* 4.7.
[62] Luigi Franco Pizzolato, "L'amicizia in Sant'Agostino e il *Laelius* di Cicerone," VC 28 (1974), 862–63.
[63] Stewart-Kroeker, *Pilgrimage*, 204.

grudges. To be sure, people in conventual communities—living in close quarters—were likely to be mulish, for they could not easily escape companions who had offended them. In such circumstances, forgiveness prompted by humility was critical, if fellowship was to survive a quarrel. So one might reasonably infer that what Pizzolato depicts as "decentering" as well as the development of "neighbor-relations" were, for Augustine, de rigueur. He would come to rely on the elect who, in turn, relied on God. Arguably, then, his own opinions about fellowship evolved. He learned to value it while mourning one friend in the company of others. Later, at Cassicacum and Thagaste, he was struck by its significance. Then at Hippo—patronizing convents, idealizing conventual life, and portraying Pelagians as arrogant apostates—he renounced self-reliance and unwaveringly plumped for humility.[64]

He was not oblivious to the dangers that excessive humility (*nimia humilitas*) posed to discipline but worried that the pervasive enmity and envy plaguing political culture might infect the alternative conventual communities he sponsored. So—though he never walked back his brief for forgiveness—he directed seasoned members of conventual communities to be firm and, while excusing younger colleagues, to keep from fawning over them.[65] Still, he never ceased repeating claims that humility stirred colleagues to reciprocal affection and that such affection held both conventual communities and ordinary congregations together. But togetherness required some degree of deference to—and some assertion of—authority. So Augustine coupled his appeals for authority with summonses to humility, which not only reiterated the bishop's conviction that humility and forgiveness were the indispensable conditions for love but also constituted his protest against taking pride in one's power. Tarsicius van Bavel rightly identifies those appeals and summonses as pivotal parts of Augustine's "social criticism."[66]

Objections may be raised that Augustine's colleagues at Cassiciacum and Thagaste were hardly opposed to leisure and

---

[64]For example, see Augustine, ep. 211.14.
[65]Augustine, *reg.*2 6.3.
[66]Tarsicius Jan van Bavel, "Rule for the Community," in *Saint Augustine*, ed. van Bavel and Bernard Bruning (Brussels: Augustinian Historical Institute, 2007), 42–43 and van Bavel, *Communauté*, 37–38.

that their "retreats" would not have been possible without patrons providing places and subsidies, patrons—Augustine included—who had been beneficiaries of the societies criticized. Be that as it may, when Augustine later formulated caveats and rules for his conventual alternatives to extramural routines, he stipulated that some sense of estrangement or exile ought to be prerequisite for entrance. At the very least, persons aspiring to join friends in those fellowships would know that what was valued there was radically different from values pervasive in commercial and political cultures. Yet, as Augustine explained, differences were sometimes underappreciated or misconstrued. For example, entrants from the lower tiers of society, seemingly well suited by habits, skills, and dispositions to assist with the menial tasks required for community maintenance, came expecting to be pampered (*pasci atque vestitur voluerunt*). Augustine learned as well that affluent entrants shared that expectation and came minimally, if at all, prepared for a life in mixed company. Still, he believed that most would soon prize humility, compassion, and their companions' dedication to the well-being of the convents.[67]

Augustine wanted parishioners as well as persons enjoying the fellowship of alternative communities to appreciate how difficult it was to behave as pilgrims—exiles from their celestial home and aliens in their terrestrial cities. His sermons commended to congregations the values that, theoretically, made alternative conventual communities work and that might be adapted to accommodate worldly persons looking for spiritual uplift. He preached humility and frequently deployed a flurry of passages from sacred texts to stress the disciples' and apostles' abhorrence of arrogance. He once digressed to remind "the first" that, *sub specie aeternitatis*, they were no better than "the last." Although prosperity might suggest otherwise to the prosperous, God had supplied clues to disabuse them of their sense of superiority. Augustine located one that nearly all auditors would likely have associated with their experiences, although he set it in a sermon, the principal purpose of which was to ridicule many Manichees' idea that only a second, sinister deity could have conjured up fleas and flies. Augustine's answer: one God

---

[67]Augustine, *op. mon.* 25; Augustine, *reg2* 3.3-4 and 5.2; Augustine, *en. Ps.* 99.10 and 125.15.

created pests as well as the people they pestered. The powerful, prosperous, and arrogant—just as those they considered inferior—were on a harrowing journey through this world, which God not only graced with grand creatures but also infested with less-than-pleasant ones. A single deity, responsible for all corporeal existence—for fleas, flies, pachyderms, and people—favored complexity for a reason, reminding the arrogant to keep their vulnerabilities in mind and to be humbled by such self-knowledge.[68]

In this instance, Augustine's pastoral lesson fit snugly with the polemical, but he tended to preach humility and compassion most emphatically when he perceived parishioners' faith in God's benevolent intent wanted reviving. On occasion, his appeal was conspicuously personal: *nolo salvus esse sine vobis*; I do not want to be saved without you.[69] Several roughly similar overtures surface in his correspondence sent to establish what could be called epistolary communities for the exchange of exegesis, consolation, and exhortation.[70] He trusted that fellowship would be sufficiently robust to enable correspondents and parishioners to endure disappointments gracefully.[71] Joseph Clair's fine study of such texts has Augustine charting a course for correspondents and congregants well shy of the renunciation expected specifically of members of his alternative, compassionate, conventual communities and—as it happens—a course of conduct much less rigorous than the one a few ascetic Pelagians were known to commend. As was his habit, Augustine tried to meet both polemical and pastoral challenges

---

[68] Augustine, *Io ev.tr.* 1.15 (*cognose qui es*). For Augustine, the faithful were tested in much more dramatic ways as well. Within a century of having gotten the attention and allegiance of Roman political authorities—whose ancestors had been dismissive, at best, and intermittently hostile—the Christians watched the empire disintegrate and its capital in the West "fall." Augustine's efforts to translate setbacks into lessons about humility and vulnerability animate some of his early fifth-century correspondence and one sermon that famously grapples with the ramifications for religion of Rome's fate. See Augustine, *exc.urb.* 1-4.
[69] Augustine, s. 17.2.
[70] For Augustine's early correspondence with Nebridius, see Lancel, *Augustin*, 189–94. For his efforts to establish epistolary "communities" based—as were the friendships at Cassiciacum and Thagaste—on a devotion to study and, after the Pelagians circulated their ideas, on opposition to them, consult Alfons Fürst, *Augustins Briefwechsel mit Hieronymus* (Münster: Aschendorf, 1999), 225–28.
[71] Augustine, *en. Ps.* 129.4: *caritas portat onera*.

simultaneously. The course he mapped demanded a degree of detachment. To follow it, ordinary Christians were to practice what Clair calls "mellow virtues," related to—yet "more mellow" than—the virtues of renunciation and reorientation Augustine expected of pilgrims. Searching the premises, then—sermons and correspondence—one could make a case that he envisioned a religion in which all the faithful were pilgrims, though some among them had become stragglers, slowed by their diminished, yet still ghoulishly astir, obsessions with possessions. But to prove that Augustine had a multitiered approach to Christian piety is difficult, for, as Clair concedes, he appears to have asked all Christians to refer the use of resources and affections "toward the highest ethical task of loving God."[72]

That this "highest task" would be more easily completed in the alternative conventual communities Augustine enthusiastically backed seems incontestable. For, in theory, no malice should have surfaced where the faithful were bent on encountering "the invisible God loved in visible" others—where, as James McEvoy reconstructs the fellowship, "fraternal charity bec[ame] the path of advancement [and] surest test of [one's] acquisition of wisdom." Augustine presumed that a select few would follow that path, setting aside their lust to be first. And that set-aside was the sacrifice drawing companions closer together and closer to martyrs whose supreme sacrifices for their faith attested God's love for creation.[73]

For Augustine, government officials would always be closer to persecutors than to his faith's martyrs, whom we will reintroduce in the next chapter. So, as already noted, summonses to and justifications for his alternative communities constituted implicit "social criticism." Early Christian fellowships, Benjamin Dunning finds, possessed a "radical sense" that they formed at "the margins

---

[72]Clair, *Discerning the Good*, 78 and 111–12. Compare Clair's discussion of Augustine's exposition and commendation of "more mellow virtues" with Robert Markus's conclusions about Augustine's "vindication of Christian mediocrity," Markus, *The End of Ancient Christianity* (Cambridge: Cambridge University Press, 1992), 50–53, but note my reservations in Kaufman, "Augustine, Martyrs, and Misery," *CH* 63 (1994), 12–14.

[73]Augustine, *Io. ev. tr.* 84.2; James McEvoy, "*Anima una et cor unum*: Friendship and Spiritual Unity in Augustine," *Recherches de théologie ancienne et médiévale* 53 (1986), 86–87. Also consult van Bavel, *Communauté*, 27.

of society," yet without "radical and subversive" intent; "the alien topos," he says, was not used to "undermine . . . broader social stability in significant ways."⁷⁴ Yet Augustine's correspondence, sermons, and treatises are more explicit and, one might say, daring when they detail standard political practices. Draconian severity was occasionally required of government authorities. Justices tortured witnesses and suspects to identify and prosecute the guilty. Civic duties were not always compatible with what Christianity demanded of the devout, Augustine noted, under no illusion that a programmatic rehabilitation or renovation of reigning political culture was possible, that some disinfectant might be energetically applied to cleanse juridical protocols. It sufficed to have magistrates consider clemency in select cases. Augustine wrote several letters to that end. Two asked Vicar Macedonius to spare Donatist dissidents who fell afoul of the law, and, as we discovered at the onset, some historians suspect the letters indicate something more seemed possible to Augustine, specifically, that he would have had the vicar and other magistrates develop "an interior disposition of gentleness" and permit "the virtue of love" to influence the courts' determinations.⁷⁵ On this reading, Augustine would have had Macedonius and similarly tasked colleagues become reformers rather than refugees, in spirit. But, were we to accept that reading, the message to Macedonius would be quite different from advice Augustine offered to an unnamed magistrate in the *City of God*, who was instructed to do his duty and torture for the truth, yet to distance himself—to decathect and pray for deliverance.⁷⁶

In Augustine's view, "the virtue of love" that might make political judgments more humane was hardly comparable to the martyrs' love for God or their compassion for others. Martyrs were drunk on love. Sobriety brought self-concern and conventional courtesies into the foreground. Ruses that disguised the lust for domination pervasive in political culture were taken as real. Augustine harbored grudging

---

⁷⁴Benjamin H. Dunning, *Aliens and Sojourners: Self as Other in Early Christian Society* (Philadelphia: University of Pennsylvania Press, 2009), 60–61.
⁷⁵Augustine, ep. 153.16-19. A few historians find the makings for a Christian magistracy in the Macedonius correspondence; consult Clair, *Discerning the Good*, 98–101 and Robert Dodaro, *Christ and the Just Society in the Thought of Augustine* (Cambridge: Cambridge University Press, 2004), 206–14.
⁷⁶Augustine, *civ*. 19.6.

respect for older Romans who were more transparent about their pursuits of glory, which we repossess in the next chapter. But in his *City of God*, where he retailed that respect, and in a striking sermon on the Psalms, he contrasted glory hounds to the Christian martyrs. The martyrs were uninterested in good government or political improvement. Augustine suggested that pilgrims were the martyrs' heirs who—in spirit, if not also in alternative communities— exchanged *conventional* loves for *conventual* fellowship.[77] By that exchange they gained a supreme consolation, a foretaste of celestial love and peace. Augustine, however, goaded no bishop to retire. Indeed, from the retreat at Thagaste and from what appears to have been a clerical convent in Hippo—from which colleagues passed into positions in African churches that required some to consult with political officials—we may infer that he may have had qualms about, but volunteered no serious objections to, diocesan duties. His letters to Macedonius and Marcellinus suggest acquiescence. But the correspondence hardly compels us to amend what we have so far learned about Augustine's disillusionment with political culture and his preferences for innovation to renovation.

He never ceased resenting the business of Babylon that tempted Licentius to forget the fellowship at Cassiciacum. He "canonized the experience of Israel in Babylon" to represent "the duality of this-worldly and divine rule," Oliver O'Donovan astutely observes, although—oddly—O'Donovan thinks one can retain Augustine's insights and still "rediscover politics not as a self-enclosed field of human endeavor but as the theater of divine self-disclosure." He is rather wary and dissents from historical theologians who argue Augustine campaigned for a transformation of political culture. But, despite his dissent, O'Donovan suspects Augustine was laying the foundation for a "significant transvaluation of the structure of society."[78]

---

[77] Augustine, *en. Ps.* 35.14; Augustine, *civ.* 5.19.

[78] See Oliver O'Donovan, *The Desire of Nations: Rediscovering the Roots of Political Theology* (Cambridge: Cambridge University Press, 1996), 82–83 and O'Donovan, *Bonds of Imperfection: Christian Politics, Past and Present* (Grand Rapids: Eerdmans, 2004), 65–68, citing *civ.* 9.14 and discussing H. Richard Niebuhr's notion that Augustine "stood for a 'transformation' of human culture by Christ." Mathewes, *Republic of Grace*, 194 seems to endorse O'Donovan's suggestion that the transvaluation would lead to some transformation, inasmuch as Jesus's

O'Donovan's distinction between "significant" transvaluations and transformations is somewhat puzzling, for he appears to avoid the obvious objection that transvaluations without political transformations—without institutional or structural support—could hardly have effects that would qualify as significant. Would the transvaluations O'Donovan's Augustine advocates be comprehensive enough to pry pilgrims from their pursuits of counterfeit joys *in hoc saeculo maligno*—in this wicked world—and generate the different hope, faith, and love he commended?[79] O'Donovan explains that Augustine stopped short of proposing political transformations because his historical perspective was "foreshortened." Augustine, that is, failed to foresee what would have been "possible given the right change in attitudes." He had not survived to see the "erosion of slavery" or to witness "the birth of law-governed states." True, although one could also argue that Augustine's judgments about what O'Donovan describes as a "civilizational progress" were sound—even prescient. Servitude and lawlessness persevere. Victims and perpetrators change in time, but heirs of late antiquity's victims, the displaced and powerless, suffer wretchedly. Heirs of late antiquity's persecutors in parliaments and packs of slave traffickers hardly seem winded. The damage to dignity is as constant as ever. As for law-governed states, history amply records the triumphs of prejudice and panic over law and the development of what Giorgio Agamben calls "states of exception," wherein regimes ostensibly governed by law create and perpetuate emergencies to justify its suspension and various aberrant, abhorrent practices.[80] What Augustine saw (and foresaw so clairvoyantly) was just how remorseless, ruthless, and coarse political culture was—and would remain. He suspected transvaluations, which O'Donovan notices him encouraging, would lead the faithful to acknowledge precisely that—to see the penal character of political existence—and, ideally, would stir them

---

"render to Caesar . . . and to God" "inject[ed] instability into politics." Would Augustine have thought so?

[79] Augustine, *civ.* 18.49; 18.54.

[80] Compare O'Donovan, *Bonds of Imperfection*, 68–69 with Agamben, *Stato di eccezione*, 74–75. Also see Bernard Aspe and Muriel Combes, "Retour sur le camp comme paradigme biopolitique," *Multitudes* 1 (2001), 30–31.

to countenance degrees of disengagement that turn citizens and subjects into perceptive pilgrims.

Agamben: Refugees and rebels

Outcasts are protagonists in the series Giorgio Agamben published on the captivity of the simple, natural life force or, in terms teased from Aristotle, Zoē. It becomes "bare life" acquiring outcast status by virtue of its exclusion by political cultures. But that exclusion is also inclusion, insofar as sovereign powers, developing protocols and roles (or "forms of life") to manage life, capture, control, and constrict Zoē. Borrowing from Michel Foucault, Agamben calls captivity (in and as politically qualified life) "biopolitics." "Bare life" liberated emerges as central for his new politics (*la figura centrale della nostra storia politica*).[81]

Biopolitics robs bare life of its potential. Until stirred by some intuition of its captivity in exile, it cannot defy protocols and give chase to alternatives. In Augustine's centuries, Agamben might have passed as a Manichaean specialist. He flirts with myth. He demonstrates a fondness for etymology. His drama of captivity, escape, and regeneration, arguably rivals those of the Manichees' elites. But the questions preoccupying Agamben for decades are as real as the regimes that increasingly concentrate power and promote conformity and as countercultural resistances to consumerist euphoria and to subtle, political tyrannies. His questions—or perhaps "dilemmas" would be a better term—amount to this: how might theorists inspire languorous or simply ill-informed persons, captured and filed as "forms of life" by the fictions of sovereignty, to turn up their collars against the chilling demands of their conventional existences and to create an authentic "form of life" and become, in Agamben's terms, "unique whatevers" who cannot be biopolitically captured or appropriated (*sul modo dell'inappropriabilità*)? How, that is, might his readers be turned

---

[81] See Giorgio Agamben, *Homo Sacer: Il potere sovrano e la nuda vita* (Turin: Einaudi, 2005), 79–96; Agamben, *Mezzi senza fine*, 15–16, 56–58, 72–73 and Agamben, *Stasis: La guerra civile come paradigma politico* (Turin: Bollati Boringhieri, 2015), 20–21.

into refugees—then rebels? For citizens satisfied with the very forms of life and protocols that sovereign powers in politics and commerce use to commodify them and to dictate the character of their captivity—such citizens cannot participate in the creation of his new politics. Participation makes Agamben's refugees rebels—then pilgrims.[82]

Refugees, as exiles, fret and exit; pilgrims face forward. The term "pilgrim" appears in Agamben's extended meditations on the relationship between religious terminology and secular sovereignty. Attending to tensions that shaped early Christians' self-understanding and doctrines, Agamben ventures to explain—without naming Augustine—why the faithful came to conceive of themselves as pilgrims. In outline, his story is fairly straightforward: to disarm pagan critics who pointed out the new faith's apparent inconsistencies, theorists—later identified with the emerging orthodox version of the Christian faith—attempted to reconcile the god that gnostic Christians set well apart from the world with the god who managed its affairs. And the reconciliation's success depended on the introduction of the concepts of pilgrimage and providence to draw the deity into this world yet also to maintain the incongruity between the celestial and the terrestrial (*la sostanziale estraneità del mondo*). The faith's most influential image makers accepted divine transcendence as a given and, Agamben explains, were undeterred by the challenges involved in preventing the wholly and holy other, "the irreducibly extraneous" from becoming utterly unrelated or, possibly worse, impersonal and diffident. So orthodoxy's impresarios agilely presented the sacraments but also the faithful themselves—as pilgrims (*peregrini*)—as tokens of divine immanence, yet as indications that their faith would never be "at home" in time.[83]

Agamben seems to admire the ingenuity of emerging Christian orthodoxy's image makers. He holds the apostle Paul in especially high regard. Paul's "product" and that of his successors for the next several centuries fascinates Agamben, yet he thinks that pilgrims

---

[82]Agamben, *Altissima Povertà*, 171.
[83]See Giorgio Agamben, *Il Regno e la Gloria: Per una genealogia teologica dell'economia e del governo* (Turin: Bollati Boringhieri, 2009), 157–58 and Agamben, *Altissima povertà*, 148–49.

only imagined they were making headway toward a celestial homeland. He would have *his* pilgrims disabused of all religious confessions' "metaphysical predicate[s] and presupposition[s]," says Adam Thurschwell, who has good grounds for maintaining Agamben was opposed to sovereign power in religious as well as secular settings.[84] His "new politics" would turn religious concepts to new uses. He calls this process "profanation" and refers to it as a serious form of play.[85] But what seems especially striking is how adamantly he requires (and Augustine required) a degree of disengagement (or decathect) from the juridical apparatuses that, in Agamben's estimation—and, plausibly, in Augustine's—were symptomatic of the sinister or fallen character of political and commercial practices. Agamben refers to presumptuous National Socialist pronouncements to document how and why governments' claims to master destiny required constant mobilization. And mobilization required then, and requires now, exclusion—ethnic cleansing in one setting and more subtle, albeit still portentous, biopolitical projects and policing in others.[86] The objective is personal but also creates a new politics; as Claire Colebrook and Jason Maxwell appreciate, one must think "immanently" and, as Agamben avers, toward ends that defy juridical appropriation.[87] Churning discontent—to which we, rather than he, would give the name "rebellion"—Agamben, for his part, explicitly calls for a war of sorts waged against conventional protocols resulting in their "nullification" or "deactivation" in refugees' dispositions—if not, as yet, in deeds. But there, in such belligerent dispositions, one experiences one's "potentiality" and defies sovereign powers' efforts to reduce citizens to ciphers and promote indolence and inertia (*inattualità*) as the officially approved *modus inoperandi*.[88]

---

[84] Adam Thurchwell, "Specters of Nietzsche: Potential Futures for the Concept of the Political in Agamben and Derrida," *Cardozo Law Review* 24 (2003), 24–31.
[85] See Agamben's "Elogio della profanazione," in his *Profanazioni* (Rome: nottetempo, 2005), 87–88: *restituire il gioco alla sua vocazione puramente profana è un compito politico*.
[86] Agamben, *Homo Sacer*, 156–57.
[87] See Claire Colebrook and Jason Maxwell, *Agamben* (Cambridge: Polity Press, 2016), 58, commenting on Agamben's *Stato di eccezione*, 80–83.
[88] For example, see Giorgio Agamben, *L'uso dei corpi*, 334–41; Agamben, *Che cos'è un dispositivo?* (Rome: Nottetempo, 2006), 26–27; and Agamben, *Communità che viene* (Turin: Einaudi, 1990), 31.

Dispositions are the sites for Agamben's politically serious form of play. Sovereign powers are too well fortified to be casually disassembled. And regime changes simply replace one set of insidiously treacherous apparatuses with another. Magistrates justify emergency detentions, deportations, and worse; they intimidate, marginalize, kennel or kill threats to their sovereignty by appealing to necessity. Looking for instances of such unimaginable cruelty, Agamben found one close at hand, the Nazi regime in which, he explains, biopolitics, which captures Zoē, turns into "thanatopolitics," which eventually extinguishes it.[89] The turn was not unprecedented. But few examples are as well—one might say, as obsessively—documented. In 1933, Hitler passed a set of laws for "the protection of the hereditary health of the German people" and, creating that "people," in effect, also created a non-Aryan population, proximity to which supposedly was sure to pollute "*the* people." Official surveillance became increasingly comprehensive. Yet the Nazis went further. Still, their preliminary tactics were not unlike security measures segregating by race, religion, immigration status, and political opinions—branding, isolating, and victimizing "populations" to protect *the* people and, Agamben adds, to protect "the biopolitical machine."[90]

So sovereign powers, in Agamben's depiction of their reach and ruthlessness, suspend or obliterate with impunity norms that O'Donovan's anthem for "law-governed states" unreservedly celebrates.[91] States of exception and their treachery are rhetorically—and crucially—braced by the reigning concepts of duty, by all the trappings of patriotism, and by adroitly orchestrated appeals to emergency, necessity, and civility. Promotion is the proper business of the magistracy secretly working to justify tyranny, whatever concessions sovereign powers seem to make to human rights discourses and democracy.[92] Agamben says that exception has become unexceptional; exception is the rule, internalized but—as

---

[89]Giorgio Agamben, *Quel che resta di Auschwitz: L'archivio e il testimone* (Turin: Bollati Boringhieri, 1998), 78.
[90]Agamben, *Quel che resta di Auschwitz*, 79–80; Agamben, *Stato di eccezione*, 35–36; and Agamben, *Mezzi senza fine*, 35–41.
[91]Agamben, *Stato di eccezione*, 111.
[92]Agamben, *L'uso dei corpi*, 266: *lavora segretamente*.

necessity requires—externally enforced.⁹³ Dispositions are where his refugee-rebel-pilgrims are born, where subjects can and should render apparatuses of sovereignty inoperative. They may come to be deactivated in disposition, should sovereignty's hold over consciousness and conscience be broken. Practicing profanation, Agamben calls this subversion and the defiant disposition it creates "messianic."⁹⁴ He writes about the result as a death to this world and a rebirth to a new redemptive life and as a messianic vocation (*klēsis*), which he associates with the messianism of the gospels and Pauline epistles. But there is some scruffiness here; Agamben's exegesis and applications are far from incontestable. Agamben adapts: "death," on his patch, nullifies the psychological effects of the juridical organization of political life (*svuotamento e nullificazione*). Having evacuated the old life of captivity, one is reborn or regenerated and wholly redeemed (*integrale riscatto*).⁹⁵

Augustine adapted as well, exploiting the biblical imagery of death and rebirth to explain how pilgrims become aware of their estrangement and why, self-consciously, they should accept their fate as sojourners. He lavished exposition on God's part in sinners' dying and redemptive rising, particularly after he flagged as pernicious the Pelagians' confidence that self-discipline and regeneration—as he construed it—had less to do with God's mercy and grace than with the would-be Christian's strenuous moral effort.⁹⁶ Augustine pored over and answered the Pelagian elaborations of their faith because he believed that their partisans, growing arrogant, would risk salvation—their salvation and, most reprehensibly, the salvation of their impressionable auditors. Agamben seems as urgent, devoting ink and energy to his many repudiations of culturally imposed "forms of life." Eternal damnation is not at stake for him as he sifts apparatuses that purportedly limit human freedom and obscure human potential, but his narrative excursions to Auschwitz, which dramatize the degradation leading all too often to the acceptance of one's juridically determined identity in states of exception, look

---

⁹³Agamben, *Stato di eccezione*, 19.
⁹⁴Giorgio Agamben, *Il tempo che resta: Un commento alla Lettera ai Romani* (Turin: Bollato Boringhieri, 2000), 91–92; and Agamben, *Homo Sacer*, 62.
⁹⁵Agamben *Il tempo che resta*, 35.
⁹⁶For example, see Augustine, ep. 157.19-21.

calculated to alert readers oblivious to the extremes to which states of exception tend and to the abhorrent consequences of readers' acquiescence or indifference.[97] According to Agamben, sovereign powers in states of exception cannot abide subjects ("singularities" or "alternative whatevers" in his lexicon), who refuse to conform and accept as natural the protocols defining and dictating conditions of belonging to one or another subset of the societies over which those powers preside. Noncompliance becomes desecration.[98] Agamben contends submission and conformity "inscribe life" into the state, redefining "person" as "citizen." Fascism and Nazism, he notes, were particularly efficient at just that.[99] Arguably, Agamben makes nonconformity and self-sufficiency heroic alternatives to groupthink. Anarchist? Solipsist? Some of his more ambiguous statements seem to leave him not only without citizenship and conditions of belonging but also without an association of any sort. Nonetheless, other statements allow us to frame a rejoinder to his many critics on this count, specifically, to reconcile his summons to subjects to become free, unique, alternative whatevers or singularities (*l'essere qualunque; l'essere qual-si-voglia*; and *singolarità qualunque*) with his interest in communal expressions of compassion and with what he hopes for and expects from "a coming community."[100] The former, his admiration for communal alternatives, which we (and he) encountered studying Augustine, arrests attention first.

---

[97]Agamben, *Quel che resta di Auschwitz*, 44: *Auschwitz è precisamente il luogo in cui lo stato di eccezione coincide perfettamente con la regola e la situatizione estrema diventa il paradigma stesso del quotidiano.*
[98]Giorgio Agamben, *La communità che viene* (Turin: Einaudi, 1990), 59–60: *la singolarità qualunque che . . . declina . . . ogni identità e ogni condizione di'appartenenza, è il principale nemico della stato.* For the customary translations of *la singolarità qualunque* and *quodlibet ens*, consult Yoni Molad, "Whatever Singularity," in *The Agamben Dictionary*, ed. Alex Murray and Jessica Whyte (Edinburgh: Edinburgh University Press, 2011), 201–4. Professor Ronney Mourad of Albion College suggested the alternative I prefer, given Agamben's sense that emancipation requires goodwill and good cheer (the *libet—libenter*—in *quodlibet*). This, of course, contrasts with Augustine's *libido dominandi*, the will, longing (lusting) to subjugate. For the podcast of my discussion of Augustine and Agamben with Professor Mourad, see http://ultimateconcerns.org/this-wicked-world, a segment of a series he originated, accessed January 29, 2017.
[99]Agamben, *Homo sacer*, 161–62.
[100]Agamben, *La communità che viene*, 1–2.

Sifting alternatives for a form of life that protests the forms of life prescribed by and prevalent in sacred as well as secular cultures, Agamben chooses a route to Augustine that passes through mendicant religious orders in the thirteenth century, specifically, Spiritual Franciscans who argued that sublime poverty (*altissima povertà*) did not preclude their using necessary objects. Agamben admits that the church's jurists scripted cogent responses but shingles with superlatives his account of the Spirituals' defiance of church officials and their allies among conservative mendicants.[101] The Spirituals' claim that their use of resources did not imply ownership was formulated as part of an indictment of the church's wealth. The opposition's insistence that usage implied ownership was meant to discredit the Spirituals' sense that only they were qualified to be Jesus's followers owing to their *altissima* poverty. And, of course, the opposition sought as well to justify the church's and other mendicants' accumulation of endowments. Spirituals' defiance and their withering criticism of ecclesial and monastic protocols endeared them to Agamben. But they would not have won over Augustine. One can imagine him criticizing as arrogant their efforts to reprise what they took to have been apostolic practices. If not arrogant, the Spirituals' initiatives surely would have seemed unrealistic to Augustine, pastor to ordinary parishioners preoccupied with providing for their families. All was not quite as it appeared, he averred, when Jesus proposed that camels might pass through the eyes of needles more readily than affluent persons would enter heaven; only a flawed exposition and application would have Jesus sanctioning strict, uncompromising renunciations. Augustine's take: Jesus was explaining that the passage to the celestial city was hard to negotiate for those who cared inordinately for what was inessential for survival—for *superflua*—because a fondness for excess prevented the faithful from cultivating an ardent affection for God (*non amat multum qui amat Deum*).[102]

Yet as a founder and patron of communal alternatives to sects and other societies in late antiquity, Augustine did interest Agamben and fit with his interests in the Spiritual Franciscans' form of life. For,

---

[101] Agamben, *Altissima povertà*, 148: *piú radicalmente degli altri movimenti; forma di vita un element radicalmente eterogeno alle istituzioni e al diritto.*
[102] Augustine, *Io. ev. tr.* 40.10.

despite Augustine's solicitude for parishioners compelled to spend, sell, and save to care for their families, he told the faithful attracted to conventual alternatives to forsake mine and thine and share their resources. Agamben's intersection with Augustine's *Rule* could have come off badly as a confrontation rather than a collaboration of sorts. He might well have taken Augustine's instructions as an unconscionable juridical intrusion. Had Augustine simply added to the forms of life that sovereign powers conventionally imposed on "bare life"? Not so, Agamben says, citing Augustine's directive that conventuals *not* consider the provisions in his *Rule* as a juridical apparatus (*non . . . come un dispositivo legale*). Agamben's Augustine was not looking to subject pilgrims to apparatuses or protocols. Agamben sees a world of difference between the rules for Augustine's conventuals and those for citizens in the fifth or twenty-first centuries, although it is not clear why. It seems to have been enough for Agamben that Augustine advised members of his alternative community in Hippo to conform to its rules—its unique form of life—freely.[103]

Spiritual Franciscans, among the mendicant orders, seem to Agamben to follow both the spirit and the letter of Augustine's *Rule*. He depicts them as refugees whose uncomplicated form of life enacted their founder Francis's dream. But he believes that apologists for their poverty and practices made a terrible mistake, citing juridical precedents for the distinction between use and ownership rather than questioning the validity of the legal definition of poverty. He would have had them concede that their practices were outside the law. The poverty they proposed—just as the use without private ownership Augustine commended—was an alternative *forma vivendi*. It was and is, Agamben says, messianic, a form of life that attests the poverty of accepted commercial and political forms of life.[104]

We have already noted—and Agamben never wearies of repeating—that commercial and political protocols channel subjects into prescribed forms of life. Spectacles, he claims, echoing Guy Debord, reinforce the captivity. To end their capture and avoid recapture, refugee-pilgrims must fashion alternatives and become

---

[103] Agamben, *Altissima povertà*, 41–42.
[104] Agamben, *Altissima povertà*, 168–69 and 175.

alternative whatevers impervious to sovereign powers' massive manipulation (*massicciamente*).[105] Staging areas for such efforts during the last half century included communitarian countercultural experiments, but advantages associated with conformity took their toll, dousing enthusiasms for nonconformity. Earlier, and for centuries, religious sects represented alternatives, but Agamben, surveying the history of some, saw that sects had compromised and became churches before and after mendicants emerged. He imagines that all conventional religious institutions would dismiss—as impulsive as well as disruptive—his summonses to captives to live messianically as alternative whatevers. As part of his discussion of insurgent "means without ends," he complains that churches clot what is messianic and liberating in their confessions (*congelare*), namely, the call to shape a new politics for their new poleis.[106]

Augustine's effort to organize alternative communities in Milan, Cassiciacum, Thagaste, and Hippo—and remarks in his sermons, correspondence, and several treatises—may be taken as encouragement to imagine a form of life distinct from those imposed in the terrestrial city. The next chapter looks more closely at those remarks, but we already know that he pressed his parishioners to live uncomfortably with the compromises they made to gain some measure of material security. *That* Augustine would appeal to Agamben, but Christianities in the twentieth and twenty-first centuries seem to him to have demonstrated little or no interest in creating or maintaining the conditions he sets for awakening human potential. Unlike Augustine, that is, the impresarios of contemporary religions are docile. Clerical and lay leaders in the West, Agamben complains, either subscribe to temporal protocols or are indifferent. They challenge, if any, only the most loathsome and barbarous elements of policy. Even then, they prefer to let their dissent marinate interminably in committees rather than to turn up the heat publicly. And they invariably shy away from resolutely advocating a deactivation of practices that ensnare ordinary others and preserve the disjunction between humanity and statist

---

[105] Agamben, *La communità che viene*, 34–35.
[106] Agamben, *Mezzi senza fine*, 104–5: *concludendo col diritto un compromesso duraturo la Chiesa ha congelato l'evento messianico*. Also see Giorgio Agamben, *La chiesa e il Regno* (Rome: Nottetempo, 2010), 14–15.

organizations (*disgiunzione incolmabile*).[107] Meanwhile, sovereign powers, Agamben says, are astoundingly resourceful; governmental reach (Michel Foucault coined the term "governmentality" to refer to it) becomes nearly irresistible.[108] In Agamben's world, sovereign powers' apparatuses are everywhere, and "the governmental machine" is what divine providence once was, ubiquitous—to catastrophic effect.[109]

May we suppose Augustine would have approved of the importance Agamben awarded temperamental deactivation and would have disapproved—with Agamben—of the government's tight grip on citizens' imaginations? We began to answer that question early in this chapter and will continue in the next. Perhaps it suffices here to remember that his Jerusalem was captive to the business of Babylon. Political advantage and commerce determined citizens' convictions. The elect, pilgrims enroute to the celestial city, needed to reassess their attachments to this world and to refocus their imaginations on their ultimate destination. But Augustine's church was *permixta*; no one could be sure which parishioners were wheat and which were chaff—hypocrites. Spasms of self-doubt were natural. Knowing his alternative communities had not always inspired an unrelenting devotion to fellowship, learning, and—later—love of God, Augustine would have appreciated Agamben's admission that communities able to empower subjects to define and realize their potential had yet to find a mind capable of compellingly conceptualizing them (*attende ancora la mente*).[110] Without relinquishing his certainty about the celestial city's existence or about contributions his church and conventual communities could make keeping pilgrims heading toward it, Augustine granted that specifics about the faithful's fate on the far side of their graves were few and quite imprecise. His mind, turning back from the frontier between time and eternity, he confided, was in no position to pronounce authoritatively on every matter pertaining to that

---

[107] Agamben, *Mezzi senza fine*, 72.
[108] Agamben, *Il Regno e la Gloria*, 230.
[109] Agamben, *Che cos'è un dispositivo*, 34–35: *in ogni ambito della vita. . . . [L]a macchina governamentale . . . ha assunto su di sé l'eredità di un governo provvidenza—alla catastrofe.*
[110] Agamben, *Mezzi senza fine*, 105.

far side.¹¹¹ On this side of the grave, he was most certain about the need to decathect. Pilgrims' hopes, faith, and loves—love for God and compassion for others—were different from ambitions and affections that characterized, and were promoted by, sovereign powers in this world. Pilgrims' finite intellects were incapable of comprehending the infinite, but what the faithful must take on faith was that they were pilgrims and that some detachment from (or deactivation of) prevailing protocols would afford them a foretaste of their celestial future.¹¹²

What followed from faith, which Augustine took to be a divine gift, was, ideally, ongoing development of those distinctive hopes, faith, and loves. He learned what preceded faith while in Milan, undertaking an intensive self-interrogation that led to his disenchantment with political culture. When he reported this in his *Confessions*, he ascribed his progress on that course to God. None could swagger to the knowledge that creatures were coddled captives in Babylon until—as refugees therefrom, temperamentally, as pilgrims—the faithful acknowledged the different hopes and loves they derived from the faith that God awakened within them. God worked within to prompt humility and compassion as well as faith.¹¹³ As Luigi Alici remarks, Augustine assumed such presence or grace came as a shock, the spectacular benefits of which poured forth from the pilgrims' love of God into their compassion for others, which just might coax them to improvise or join alternative, conventual communities.¹¹⁴ Augustine supposed that the emergence of these communities, in time, would always be a work-in-progress, with progress dependent on pilgrims' resolve to be and remain reformed and, as instructed by the apostle Paul, unconformed to this world. The resolve or determination depended on God. Their

---

¹¹¹Augustine, *civ.* 22.30: *temere definire non audeo quod excogitare non valeo*.

¹¹²For example, see Augustine s. 16A.1 (*inter aeternitatem enim et tempus multum distat*) and s. 16A.13 (*Peregrini simus. Nemo terreatur; Patria hic non est*).

¹¹³One of Augustine's sermons on God's grace in the sacraments digressed (Augustine, s. 228B.2) to signal what so many of his other sermons stressed: that God also worked salvation from within.

¹¹⁴Augustine, *Io. ev. tr.* 65.1 (*innovat gentes*). In this connection, consult Luigi Alici, "*Interrogatio mea, intentio mea*: Le movement de la pensée augustinienne," in *Augustin, philosophe et prédicateur: Hommage à Goulven Madec* (Paris: Institut d'Études Augustiniennes, 2012), 379–81.

inordinate desires lured pilgrims back. Conformity or captivity was a recurring prospect. Possibly, as he relayed his certainty in his treatise on the Trinity, he recollected how or why his plans for alternative communities in Italy had come unhinged.[115] Speculation aside, we can say Augustine learned, both early and late in his pursuits of learning and leisure, that there would be no kingdom of God on earth. The faith and love attesting God's presence in (and to) the faithful, who then longed for incorruptibility hereafter, did not keep them from groaning under burdens imposed on them by their commitments in the here and now.[116]

Just as consistently, Augustine attributed exiles' and pilgrims' groaning and longing as well as their resolve to God's grace, as we see. As early as 396, shortly after becoming bishop, he insisted there could be no breakthrough to faith without a divine descent into—and presence in—human will.[117] As noted, much was left unsaid—because much could not be known—about pilgrims' ultimate destination, yet, on the matter of their inspiration, Augustine was unreserved, especially after Pelagians in Africa started circulating treatises implying creatures could love God and others aided only by the grace they received in their baptisms and with the knowledge God imparted in the law. That seemed ridiculous to Augustine. He scolded Pelagius and his admirers for having underestimated human corruptibility. And the idea that love originated without God's presence *in nobis*—as love—was a perfect specimen of self-inflating make-believe, a belief that attested Pelagians' impiety and incredulity while, in effect, maligning Christianity's martyrs, who proved to Augustine that humility and faith were inseparable.[118]

It may not be quite accurate to state, as Jérôme Lagouanère does, that Pelagians forced Augustine "to systematize" a theology of grace, but they definitely gave him the occasion and incentive emphatically to formulate his faith that faith itself and love were gifts from God. The Pelagians, that is, motivated him to personalize

---

[115] Augustine, *trin.* 14.14.22.
[116] Augustine, *conf.* 6.14,24: *ad suspira et gemitus et gressus ad sequendas latas et tritas vias saeculi*; Augustine, *civ.* 20.17: *qui primitias habentes Spiritus in semetipsis ingemescunt*.
[117] Augustine, *Simp.* 1.2,22.
[118] Augustine, *gr. et lib. arb.* 19.40, citing 1 Jn 3.1 and 1 Cor. 2.12. A discussion of martyrs and pilgrims follows in the next chapter.

divine providence, or to be more precise, their confidence in human initiative and endeavor prodded him to reassert what he dramatized in his *Confessions* when he vividly presented a personalized plan divinely set and staged to draw him to the faith.[119] He was altogether convinced that God was responsible for reforming some and leaving others conformed to this world. He was equally sure that the reformations of the reformed were ongoing, if precarious, affairs over which God presided. Neither certainty, however, relieved him or his colleagues of the duty to preach nonconformity. Augustine's correspondence, sermons, doctrinal elaborations, polemical treatises, personal reminiscences, and compendious *City of God* attest his diligence in pressing pilgrims to trust what sacred literature purportedly promised those who took faith as an unmerited token of God's love—and who paid forward that gift by loving others. Pastoral efforts notwithstanding, God's presence in and to the elect was the determining factor in their fate. But Agamben does not introduce a deity into what might pass as his drama of salvation. He knows churches attributed the distinctiveness of the messianic community to God's work within Christians, yet he faults churches for having adopted a juridical strategy to counter the Pelagians' contention that baptism forever sealed the redemption of the baptized. He refers to one of Augustine's anti-Pelagian treatises, although he overlooks its location of grace within pilgrims' wills, which was more mystical than juridical.[120]

Agamben does find the sources for medieval communal alternatives or movements he admires in late antiquity, where self-styled exiles led cloistered and contemplative lives. Their deactivations of prevailing statist protocols were rather tame; some of their medieval descendants were more transgressive; Agamben has them occasionally setting up or prophesying new states of exception to replace the old.[121] His illustrations are few

---

[119]Jérôme Lagouanère, "Augustin, à l'écoute de la *Prima Johannis*: La définition augustinienne de la notion de prochain," *Bulletin de littérature ecclésiastique* 113 (2012), 162–63.
[120]Agamben, *Il tempo che resta*, 115–16. Agamben's equation of the administration of grace and law seems more relevant to late medieval soteriology. For Augustine's mysticism, consult Andrew Louth, *Origins of the Christian Mystical Tradition: From Plato to Denys*, 2nd ed. (Oxford: Oxford University Press, 2007), 128–52.
[121]Agamben, *Homo Sacer*, 62.

but telling, but the correspondences between contemplation and subversion or inoperativity seem overdrawn. Moreover, his more exuberant discussions of convents' and messianic movements' independence from sovereign political and ecclesial powers require refinement.[122] But having staked out his patch, he urgently wants to draw readers in. From his perspective, they need awakening. They perform their lives or, Agamben suggests, their prescribed forms of life as extras or walk-ons (*comparse*), bereft of their power to become inoperative and therefore diminished or, worse, expendable.[123] Hence, it is understandable—if unpardonable—that imperatives related to the urgency of awakening others tempt Agamben to sacrifice some historical complexity. The task is to unmask totalitarianism. There, too, Agamben can be challenged, but it is not exactly damning to attribute his fears and alerts to "the cynicism of 1968," as Charles Mathewes does, alluding to his "near-complete innocence about real politics." What troubles Mathewes, criticizing Agamben, is something mildly more interesting—and far more common—than the cynicism among tenured radicals, something Amy Elias calls postmodern paranoia about "normativizing cultural order[s]."[124]

But the old saw still cuts: paranoia does not necessarily mean that what is excessively feared is unreal. Social Democrats' anxieties about normativizing cultures in Germany during the early 1930s were branded as extravagant and irrational. When C. Wright Mills feared standards of "the power elite" in the 1950s amounted to "a higher immorality," which trickled down into ordinary behavior, was he paranoid or prophetic; paranoid or prophetic, when marking the elite's perpetuation of a state of emergency to frighten and control the public? (Mills and his emergency [the Cold War] look like precursors of Agamben and the state of exception juridically suspending procedural protections to protect citizens

---

[122]For example, see Agamben, *Il Regno e la Gloria*, 270–74 and Agamben, *Altissima povertà*, 143–49.
[123]Agamben, *Homo Sacer*, 93–94, for expendability; Agamben, *Nudità*, 69–70, for walk-ons and forms of life that rob subjects of their potential to be defiant and declare inoperativity and impotentiality (*inoperositá; impotenza*).
[124]Charles Mathewes, "Feasting on Glory," *Political Theology* 14 (2013), 69–70; Amy Elias, "Paranoia, Theology, and Inductive Style," *Soundings* 86 (2003), 282.

in sovereign powers' never-ending war on terror.[125]) Thirty years later, Alasdair MacIntyre's protests against the decline of civility and morality in the United States were thought shrill, mis-timed, and especially over the top when he identified parallels between the Roman Empire's decadence—along with western Europe's slide into "the Dark Ages"—with the trajectory of government in his time in which the barbarians, he said, were "not waiting beyond the frontiers [but] have already been governing us for quite some time." When MacIntyre's misgivings were described in some quarters as ravings, he added that his countrymen's "lack of consciousness" of barbarians within—the descendants of Augustine's glory hounds and forerunners of Agamben's sovereign powers, perhaps— "constituted" [their] "predicament." MacIntyre mentioned that, in late antiquity, some became conscious of a similar predicament and devised new forms of community, the very conventual alternatives Augustine promoted and Agamben admires. Apparently referring to secular improvisations, MacIntyre's paranoid (?) or prophetic (?) screed against individualism says that "what matters at this stage [1981] is the construction of local forms of community within which . . . moral life can be sustained through the new dark ages . . . already upon us."[126]

MacIntyre's barbarians and his "local forms of community" seem a long way from the "hopeful" and "democratic" citizenship that faith in civic humanism promotes. Agamben strenuously objects to the equation of "citizen" with "human," foregrounding the humanity of refugees. The marginalization and exclusion of refugees, he contends, referring to Europe's internment camps into the 1990s, turn citizens into barbarians. He suggests that there is a perfect affinity between efforts to confine exiles who could be neither assimilated nor repatriated and the concentration-extermination camps fifty years before (*una filiazione perfettamente reale*). He understates the problem at one point, describing the confined as

---

[125] For Social Democrats' anxieties in the 1920s and 1930s, see Richard J. Evans, *The Coming of the Third Reich* (New York: Penguin, 2003), 277–83 and Hannah Arendt, *The Origins of Totalitarianism* (New York: Harcourt, 1994), 258–66; for the higher immorality in the 1950s, see C. Wright Mills, *The Power Elite* (Oxford: Oxford University Press, 2000), 292–97, 350–61.
[126] Alasdair MacIntyre, *After Virtue: A Study in Moral Theory* (Notre Dame: University of Notre Dame Press, 1984), 263.

"a disquieting element," yet quickly passes to the xenophobia that betrays the brutality of the sociopolitical reality of modern states, which, Agamben argues, puts the very concept of citizenship into crisis (*mette in crisi; mette in crisi radicale*). An occasional observation savors of amateurish optimism—calling to mind what Mathewes maintains about his "innocence"—as when he refers to the imminent undoing or dismantling (*scardina*) of statist protocols and the likelihood that ethnonationalism's many celebrations of citizenship can be effectively undermined. But Agamben does an effective job positioning his analysis as a preface to "a new political history," in which his emphasis on the centrality of the refugee as well as his unmasking of the constructed character of "citizenship" and the "citizen" enable us to clear the field, as he desires (*sgmobrare il campo*), and mark a beginning of the end of sovereignty's creation and captivity of life.[127]

Clearing the field is demanding work. The beginning of the end of captivity is only a beginning. Even when select social roles and protocols are dismantled, the concept of citizenship so crucial to biopolitics in the twentieth and twenty-first centuries is robust and well defended by pageants, spectacles, oaths, and acclamations. Apparatuses that disguise its deficiencies, shield it from criticism, and make citizenship sacrosanct are principal targets of operations that Agamben variously describes as deactivation, nullification, and destitution (*una destituzione del dispositivo della cittadinanza*).[128] Citizenship, however, comes with privileges and plays upon individuals' seemingly insatiable thirsts for recognition. Anthropometric techniques long used to monitor criminals now give citizens markers that reassure them they count—markers in their purses or secured in data banks. Every chip and code lugs subjects deeper into captivity; self-surrender masquerades as self-sufficiency.[129]

Agamben's call for deactivation is unrealistic, unless, of course, the decathect is covert. Even then, though, his iconoclasm astounds, and it is pointless to ask him to furnish explicitly formulated,

---

[127]See Agamben, *Mezzi senza fine*, 25–27, where the refugee, *un element cosi inquietante*, becomes *la figura centrale della nostra storia politica*.
[128]Agamben, *L'uso dei corpi*, 346–47.
[129]Agamben, *Nudità*, 77–79.

comprehensive replacements for the conventional certainties and values he would sabotage. As we now know, he countenances only a selective, unconventional use of concepts, protocols, and apparatuses—use that allegedly will serve the liberation of alternative whatevers or singularities and the emergence of alternative communities, the contours of which have yet to be determined. And this "profanation" purportedly liberates both the user and what gets used. For Agamben, this emancipation amounts to a messianic reappropriation whereupon everything becomes new (*ecce sono diventate nuove*).[130]

He does not elaborate. He stumps readers looking for bare life, liberated, to take some definite—rather than a "whatever"—form. He makes what Sergei Prozorov terms a "turn towards experimentation," and the experiments continually emerge rather than settle as a well-articulated form of life. "Communitarians" who, as Gerard Delanty says, "are interested less in spontaneous, anti-structural community than in a normative theory of political community," will surely grow impatient milliseconds after reading Agamben proposing only that profanation ought to restore possibilities denied by protocols and apparatuses that captivate and capture subjectivity.[131] The turn toward experimentation oddly resembles nostalgia; although, making the turn, Agamben's tracts refuse to stipulate the results, save to say that, having detonated the dispositions packing persons into conventional forms of life (or social roles), his "new politics" opens possibilities for virtuous friendships.[132]

Augustine was also eager to find foundations for friendships of this sort, searching, as we have seen, in biblical depictions of a love distinct in origin and telos from the loves of this world. His sermons

---

[130] Agamben, *Il tempo che resta*, 31–32.
[131] Agamben, *Che cos'è un dispositivo*, 30–31; Sergei Prozorov, *Agamben and Politics* (Edinburgh: Edinburgh University Press, 2014), 182–83: "Agamben proposes what appears to be a self-consciously *minoritarian*, if not outright 'bohemian', form of life that can hardly be expected to be replicated across the whole of society, simply because the attraction of profanatory experiments and playful subversions of the existing apparatuses is far from self-evident." But such was not Agamben's expectation. "Everything becomes new" in the dispositions of a few. Gerard Delanty, *Community* (Routledge: London, 2003), 73, sifts communitarians' interest in norms.
[132] Agamben, *L'amico* (Rome: Nottetempo, 2007), 13.

show he was not averse to looking for leverage to reshape those other loves, but he imagined that the cavernous character of late imperial and provincial government made comprehensive political reform implausible. So he was resigned to corruption yet remained indignant—critical of the lust for mastery that made it pervasive.[133] Augustine conceded that distinctions in legal status between slave and free—as well as other categories that denoted (or masked) inequities—should be observed, yet he trusted that faith would take away (Agamben would say "deactivate") whatever divided pilgrims, spiritually and ruinously.[134]

Augustine and Agamben stalk alternatives to forms of life and ambitions encouraged by the powers that be. Unlike MacIntyre, who figured that barbarism might diminish ("we are not entirely without grounds for hope"), Augustine urged pilgrims and Agamben directs readers to harbor hopes quite different from those that look for sovereign powers' inhumanity lastingly to give way to civilization. Refugee-pilgrims ought to hope for something that far exceeds civility. In the public realm, as Agamben repossesses it, there are but tiny chances for improvement as long as sovereign powers' protocols and pageants, human rights discourses, and even much of leftist dissent perpetuate the illusion that an "upstanding democratic citizen" will act prudently and avoid radically challenging the captivity to which citizens—unlike refugee-pariah-pilgrims—have become habituated.[135] And the pressures to naturalize, repatriate, or exterminate refugees prove to Agamben that there is no space in the conventionally organized political order for the vitality and perceptiveness of unique whatevers.[136] Still, the temptation to transcend ought to be avoided. One cannot be in an utterly different space (*un altrove*). Deactivation and nullification are "messianic" without leaping to some more satisfactory existence; instead, they create "a zone" in which the passing of this world can be experienced, Agamben obscurely explains, where the differences between the immanent and transcendent are imperceptible or

---

[133]Augustine, *civ.* 5.15-16 and 14.28; Augustine, ep. 151.4 and ep. 236.1.
[134]Augustine, *exp. Gal.* 28: *differentia ista . . . ablata est ab unitate fidei.*
[135]See Agamben, *Che cos'è un dispositivo,* 32, for *la maschera ipocrita del buon cittadino democratico.*
[136]Agamben, *Mezzi senza fine,* 24.

"indiscernible."[137] As for other "zones," the biopolitical project completely colonizes "normal," collective "and thus political" life.[138]

Augustine also commended achieving perspective on the passing of this world. Pilgrims understood what this meant for their bearing in this world—their undeclared wars on obsessions with possession—for their celestial rewards. Their hope for those was sustained by experiences of commiseration or compassion—by a love for others inspired by pilgrims' love for the love of God present—and extended—in those others' love for God and in *their* compassion.[139] God's love for creation was the groundwork. Augustine trusted it to prime what Jérôme Lagouanère describes as a radical yet apolitical transformation of interpersonal relations.[140] Interpersonal relations are not nearly as prominent in the experimentation and emancipation Agamben commends. For the love of and for God pulsing through the compassion Augustine urges, Agamben substitutes a love for being, stirred in subjects by friendships that, in turn, stir an otherness in themselves. This internal alterity generates an intensity, which ends their complacency and which Agamben identifies as a political potency. Nonetheless, in terms that would have appealed to Augustine, Agamben sifts Louis Massignon's efforts to extend "the hospitality of Christ" in the conventual community he assembled in Cairo in the early 1930s. For Agamben, hospitality of this sort requires readers to ratchet up awareness and become intensely empathic refugees. He suggests as much, depicting alternative whatevers as "expatriates" who "deport," exile, or extend themselves into the sentiments of others in his "community to come."[141]

Agamben "deports" himself differently; he ranges widely. Coffins are no barriers as long as their occupants left terms and ideas that

---

[137] Agamben, *Il tempo che resta*, 30: *una zona di assoluta indiscernibilità tra immanenza e transcendenza.*
[138] Agamben, *Homo Sacer*, 143.
[139] See, inter alia, Augustine, *civ.* 18.54; *trin.* 8.8; *ep. Io. tr.* 12; and *exp. Gal.* 43–45.
[140] Jérôme Lagouanère, "L'amour du proachain dans Augustin d'Hippone," *Augustinianum* 54 (2014), 155–56.
[141] Agamben, *La communità che viene* 17–18: *espatriarsi in lui tale qual è per offrir ospitalià a Christo nella sua stessa anima.* For "deportation" and internal alterity, see Agamben, *L'amico*, 17–18.

can be turned to advantage. He borrows from Pindar's poetry—composed centuries before the Pauline epistles he shuffles into his remake of messianism—and from postmodernism's prolific theorists. We have already noted his considerable debt to Michel Foucault; Walter Benjamin's comments on Carl Schmitt's political theology gave Agamben insights that memorably associate the state of exception with prevailing political practices and with the protocols enforced by sovereign powers.[142] He occasionally visits with Augustine and with the third subject of our story, Hannah Arendt, finding and featuring the form of life the former configured for alternative communities of pilgrims and another form of life the latter furnished for pariahs. Agamben draws from their configurations and furnishings—from the virtues they celebrate—although he refuses to impose them (or best practices) on his alternative whatevers. The coming being and coming community must be whatever they will be.[143] The becoming of both will be unfinished business until refugee-rebel-pilgrims decathect, ending their captivity to sovereign powers. For now, we can only imagine that Augustine and Agamben would concur and have readers release their grip on conventional ambitions—which, in effect, have a firm hold over them—because the hopes of hopeful *citizens* are either too restricted by sovereign powers' protocols and spectacles (Agamben) or too constricted by self-love (Augustine) to conjure radical alternatives. In the next chapter, we shall see that Augustine's estimation of Romans' pageants, spectacles, protocols, and politics—as extensions of *amor sui* and of humans' lust for domination—justifies teaming him with Agamben and, as the chapter after argues, with Hannah Arendt as well.

---

[142]Giorgio Agamben, "Il Messia e il sovrano: Il problema della legge in W. Benjamin," in *Anima e paura: Studi in onore di Michele Ranchetti*, ed. Bruna Bocchini Camaiani and Anna Scattigno (Macerata: Quodlibet, 1998), 11–12.
[143]Agamben, *La comunità che viene*, 3: *L'essere che viene è l'essere qualunque.*

2

Glory, Glory

Agamben—the Coming Overcoming

Agamben and Augustine acknowledged that the apostle Paul influentially auditioned alternatives to prevailing forms of life in Roman Palestine. For Augustine, Paul's resistance to social roles was part of his politics of grace; God's love replaced the law and made new poleis possible. For Agamben, the apostle's resistance amounted to inoperativity and was more than a part of his Paul's new political perspective; it was at the very center of Paul's understanding of messianic time, the special quality of which could be realized before the afterlife whenever the faithful deactivated juridical protocols.[1]

Controversial philosopher Alain Badiou agrees. Badiou's Paul refused to let the available statist and ideological generalizations determine individuals' identities. Badiou is one of the slew of theorists who—as Agamben has—found Paul's resistance especially timely in the late twentieth century as capitalism and the media seemed increasingly to reify and commodify communitarian identities.[2] Their Paul is an apostle of "emancipatory deactivation." At this chapter's conclusion, we should be able to put Augustine in their company. He probably would have been perplexed by Agamben's advocacy of indeterminacy, as many contemporary

---

[1] Agamben, *Il Regno e la Gloria*, 271, citing 1 Cor. 9.25.
[2] Badiou, *Saint Paul: La foundation de l'universalisme* (Paris: Presses universitaires de France, 1997), 14.

critics are, yet Agamben's (and Badiou's) "deconstructive instincts" protests problematizing prevailing political values might have seemed to Augustine quite timely and congenial.³

For the trajectory of Augustine's protests was quite similar. His assessment of late Roman political culture placed the feverish pursuit of glory at its very heart, lamenting that Christians, without much coaching, became glory hounds. They were captivated by the rituals civic leaders subsidized and choreographed to gain name and fame—for adulation and acclaim.⁴ For his part, Agamben couples Carl Schmitt's comments on acclamation— public endorsements of sovereign powers—with Guy Debord's criticisms of developed countries' commodifications, which their "societ[ies] of spectacle" celebrate.⁵ What he concludes from his sources and from his usually riveting—albeit sometimes obscure—studies that range from contemporary politics to pornography is that a quest for glory dominates public life. What could be called the implements of acclamation—scepters, crowns, and thrones, which awed commoners for millennia—have long been packed away in museums, yet, Agamben claims, the media and their beneficiaries in power have found many replacements; acclamations continue in contemporary democracies. Agamben has us confronting an unprecedented "concentration . . . of the function of glory as the center of the political system." Indeed, fascist regimes proved particularly resourceful, devising "bilateral liturgies" that incited citizens to acclaim and dignify sovereign powers suffusing citizens with a sense of their glorious status and mission.⁶

A thirst for glory turned Rome from a city into an empire. Its expanse was the backdrop for the apostle Paul's and for Augustine's ministries. Badiou claims that Rome's reach inclined the apostle to

---

³For "emancipatory . . . deconstructive instincts," see Gideon Baker, "The Revolution Is Dissent: Reconciling Agamben and Badiou on Paul," *Political Theory* 4 (2013), 321–24.
⁴Augustine, *en. Ps.* 149.10.
⁵Guy Debord, *La société du spectacle*, 3rd ed. (Paris Gallimard, 1992), 26.
⁶See Agamben, *Il Regno e la Gloria*, 254–55 and 280: *In questione è nulla di meno che una nuova e inaudita concentrazione, moltiplicazione e disseminazione della funzione della Gloria come centro del Sistema politico.*

"break" with Jewish law, range beyond Jerusalem, be inclusive, and preach to all who would listen. Yet he was not the architect of a universal church. Paul preferred to "decenter" Christianity, Badiou proposes; the apostle set up cells, *noyaux* or nuclei. Such terms suggest that the scale was quite modest. Was the term "congregation" deliberately avoided? Perhaps, but the choice of *noyaux* makes the results of Paul's ministry comparable to what Augustine assembled at Cassiciacum or Thagaste. Be that as it may, Badiou guesses that Paul and other early apostles discovered what Jesus, as the curtain-raiser, had little time to learn but what Augustine perceived from the start of his career, namely, that conventicles "plunged" into an unfriendly world, became churches, mired in its affairs—that, as Badiou says, priests replaced saints.[7]

Agamben's apostle is more militant than Badiou's; his Paul was a pilgrim who plunged into the world first as persecutor then as persecuted, having interrogated the world's values and found them wanting.[8] Political life at the time, Agamben claims, was characterized by grandiose, choreographed acclamations, and their amplitude was generally disproportionate to powers that the acclaimed could actually claim.[9] For him and for his Paul, the messianic vocation was, as we now know, to annul or nullify the majesty of magisterial office, which the acclamations extolled. Paul and subsequent pilgrims radically called into question the very conditions and forms of life that defined them, calling on others to live in—but not to be of—this world. The messianic calling shifts one's perception, so that glory in this world means little. But Agamben finds it less taxing to proclaim messianism's antinomian tendencies than to specify their implications for personal and interpersonal behavior.[10]

The closest he came to such specifications were his projections for a community to come as a result of his new politics, and, as we learned at the conclusion of the previous chapter, even those projections did not come very close. Agamben makes amply clear

---

[7]Badiou, *Saint Paul*, 36–41: *le saint effacé par le prêtre*.
[8]Agamben, *Il Regno e la Gloria*, 158.
[9]Agamben, *Il Regno e la Gloria*, 204–7.
[10]See Agamben, "Il Messia e il sovrano," 16 and Agamben, *Il tempo che resta*, 28–29, citing 1 Cor. 7.29-32.

that the coming community will impose no conditions of belonging on those who belong, yet he appears to overlook what surely qualify as negative conditions. Subjects living in messianic time in Agamben's coming community will have deactivated protocols that kept them captive. They would no longer be counted among glory hounds. An absence of specifiable, determinative contents—missing representable conditions or bonds of belonging—would characterize their gatherings, as an absence of specifics, he says, characterized all but one of the grievances propelling the 1989 protests at Tiananmen Square.[11] But defiance was certainly a condition. Hence, the negative becomes a bond, most clearly when Agamben imagines the novelty of his new, coming politics (*politica che viene*), which debuts as a coming overcoming of not just statist domination but of the disciplinary and distracting strategies maintaining it.[12]

Groups and movements struggling for inclusion may constitute efforts to establish what Jenny Edkins calls a "counter-hegemony," but Agamben's discourse is unflinchingly "counter" and is hegemonic only in the sense that it intends to overrule reigning discourses, pageants, and protocols.[13] It substitutes nothing settled and specific, but its illustrations are not unimpeachable. Agamben may be looking for examples of his alternative form of life where, as he would know, it had been betrayed—among the Spiritual Franciscans, the Humiliati, and other medieval alternative movements led by Norbert of Xanten and Robert of Arbrissel, who improvised buoyantly and transparently (*lietamente; apertamente*), yet Norbert and Robert eventually accommodated authorities and settled into monasteries. Their alternatives, as Augustine's, became parts of an ecclesial status quo. Correspondences with Agamben's

---

[11] Agamben is correct, but the single conspicuous demand that dissident students be heard, a demand for dialogue with the government, was preceded and accompanied by factions' discussing specific grievances to be aired. That consensus was hard to reach about any bill of complaints can be attributed to the speed with which the mobilization took place—exceeding the students' "expectations and experience"; see Craig Calhoun, *Neither Gods nor Emperors: Students and the Struggle for Democracy in China* (Berkeley: University of California Press, 1994), 54–59, 155–87.
[12] Agamben, *La communitá che viene*, 58.
[13] Jenny Edkins, "Whatever Politics," in *Giorgio Agamben: Sovereignty and Life*, ed. Matthew Calarco and Steven DeCaroli (Stanford: Stanford University Press, 2007), 73–74.

coming community that, in effect, become the foremost enemy of the state, would have existed only if their orders (Praemonstratensians [Norbert], Fontrevault [Robert], or Augustinians) repudiated rather than set conditions for belonging. Agamben requires his alternative whatevers and coming community to disavow settled identities (*declina . . . ogni identità*). Yet he nods favorably to the above—and to the apostle Paul, whose leadership demanded their becoming prescriptive. Arguably, Agamben does as well, stipulating that a refugee-rebel-pilgrim is optimally positioned to analyze citizens' captivity. So it seems fair to ask whether parts of the plumbing need fixing before Agamben's coming overcoming comes. Probably, but his insights about the obstacles to its coming and the ways to overcome them can be used to revisit Augustine's pilgrims and his assessment of captivity in Babylon: of boasting, glory, and humility.[14]

Boasting

One of the most daunting pastoral challenges facing Augustine was to prompt, then to accelerate parishioners' disillusionment with all that the world thought glorious. Pride in one's personal achievements and one's *patria* came naturally; the pursuit of recognition was pervasive. Cities put up monuments to their patrons and gods. Only the discerning could see that name and fame meant little, Augustine lamented, and that insatiable appetites disturbed the peace of those longing for more and fearing that luck would turn and leave them with less.[15] He wished more would comprehend just that. History helped. Barriers to understanding should drop once one realizes how fortune played havoc with Rome's empire, emperors, legions, and commanders. Military and political reversals experienced in the fourth and early fifth centuries proved that anxieties attending appetites for conquest were well founded. But Augustine did concede that leading citizens' desire for glory—theirs and their empire's—was responsible, in large part, for republican and imperial Rome's growth. We shall attend to this concession shortly, because it appears

---

[14]Compare Agamben, *La communità che viene*, 60 and Agamben, *Altissima povertà*, 117.
[15]Augustine, *en. Ps.* 72.11.

to undermine his sense that exaggerated self-esteem (*iactantia*) was the devil's handiwork. Persons who attribute accomplishments to their courage and competence, failing to acknowledge God's gift of both, he said, collaborate with the devil—their arrogance being both baseless and blasphemous.[16]

Of the accomplishments that seemed most praiseworthy to Augustine, those of chaste persons were especially inspiring but seemed perilous as well. Virgins, whom he congratulated and encouraged in a treatise devoted to their sacrifices, were, he feared, teetering on the edge of arrogance. Their superior righteousness was legend. But legends tempt the legendary to believe their press. Augustine proffered advice. Virgins should think of others, whose restraint was less impressive than theirs, as exemplary in different ways. If the chaste practiced what amounted to a thought experiment as a spiritual exercise, Augustine promised that no exaggerated sense of self-worth (*ruinosa iactantia*) would wreck their reputations for restraint.[17]

Humility was well served by imagining others' virtues. Self-assurance could be inoffensive, Augustine allowed, citing David's face-off against Goliath, but presumptuous persons risked ingratitude to God for the gifts stirring them to think well of themselves.[18] In Augustine's judgment, presumption always seemed linked to a love of—and a need for—power and praise. And he believed that arrogance was not simply an affront to God; it was an obstacle for God's compassion to overcome, an obstacle for Christians' consciences trying to counter their thirst for glory, to patrol and fortify their faith's reputation, and to preserve both peace and some semblance of justice.[19] Augustine's sermons raked passages from sacred literature into his claim that it was as unwise to rely on others' praise and on one's celebrity as it was to count on the permanence of a great estate, a small trinket, or an acknowledged eminence. The world was unstable. Its only abiding characteristic, impermanence. That popularity and prestige—much as profits—go and come, often abruptly and unpredictably, should

---

[16] Augustine, *en. Ps.* 7.4.
[17] Augustine, *virg.* 53.
[18] Augustine, s. 32.3.
[19] Augustine, *civ.* 12.8.

have been obvious to students of human relations and history, Augustine argued, suggesting that no other conclusion would occur to astute observers of glory, as onlookers claimed it for persons or poleis.[20]

He wanted to be certain that catechumens became astute and informed observers. They ought to see how and why their awareness of impermanence would minimize the chances that their self-assurance came off as pride, so he alerted their instructors at the gateway to the faith that all the possessions and pleasures from which they and their students derived solace in this world were precarious. Predictably, they hoped to be undisturbed in the enjoyment of their assets; they wanted to carry their good reputations to the grave. But covetous, false friends might steal from them. Fickle crowds could withhold approval. A sudden fever (*febricula*) could kill the most affluent and influential citizen.[21] Pastoral efforts to deflate egos played up personal jeopardy. Respectability and prized possessions were—when Augustine spoke of them in some sermons—only a cough or crisis away from liquidation. Challenges to exaggerated self-esteem in his self-evidently polemical treatises took a different tack. During his nearly ten years among Manichees, he accumulated stories about their specialists' conceit and condescension and, on leaving them for Christianity, trotted out those tales to discredit the sect. Manichaean specialists, claiming to reveal the secrets of creation, to explain mysteries associated with diet and decorum, and to make Christianity more intelligible, he said dismissively, were too new, too few, and too confused to make lasting impressions. Still, he wrote venomously and at length about their crazy concepts, lewd conduct, and sedulous pursuit of celebrity.[22]

He did not underestimate the difficulty prelates had making Christianity intelligible to commoners. Parts of the Hebrews' scriptures that prefaced narratives purportedly composed by and undeniably about evangelists and apostles bewildered ordinary Christians who missed the relevance of Israelite history or the psalmist's poetry. Jesus's parables could be baffling.[23] But Bishop

---

[20] Augustine, *en. Ps.* 131.25.
[21] Augustine, *cat. rud.* 16.24-25.
[22] Augustine, *util. cred.* 14.31: *tam pauci, tam turbulenti, et tam novi.*
[23] Augustine, *mor.* 1.7.11.

Ambrose had helped Augustine make sense of scripture; Platonism made him tolerant; what Cornelius Maier calls Platonism's "cloud of unknowing" did not frighten him. But what startled him after he defected from the Manichaean sect (unless he was feigning surprise) was that its specialists appeared incapable of knowing their own unknowing.[24] They claimed to have mastered the secrets of the cosmos as well as those of Christianity. After Ambrose, he was more determined to leave and was never tempted to scamper back to their colloquies. Predictably, he considered their claim to reveal the real meaning of sacred literature an exponentially more egregious boast than any the specialists made about their insight or integrity. Critical to the emerging orthodoxy he was helping to shape were his reaffirmations of the evangelists' and apostles' understandings of Jesus's incarnation. But, to the Manichees, the genealogies in two of the gospels made no sense. Their savior had descended directly from a realm of light and could not have been a descendant of the Hebrews' King David. Deaf to such drivel, Augustine trained his artillery on what the Manichaean elite dubbed the rule of reason, which, he scoffed, none but they and credulous auditors could believe rationally defensible. He remorselessly pilloried their campaigns to discredit evangelists, apostles, and early Christians who celebrated Jesus's origin, incarnation, and passion.[25]

The Manichees' traffic in secrets gave no sign of abating in the early fifth century, by which time Augustine was busy opposing Donatists' and Pelagians' versions of Christianity he thought problematic. But he could not forget the Manichees. For while developing his defenses of God's sovereignty in his other polemical campaigns, he may well have been wary of "falling [back] completely into Manichaean anthropology," as Jason BeDuhn suspects, when calculating the presence of both sin and grace in the will of the faithful.[26] Did dualism surfacing in his anti-Pelagian tracts remind

---

[24] Augustine, *conf.* 9.4.8. For unknowing (*Wolke der Torheit*), see Cornelius Maier, "Garanten der Offenbarung: Probleme der Tradition in den ani-manichäischen Schriften Augustins," *Augustinianum* 12 (1972), 60.
[25] Augustine, *c. Faust.* 2.1-3. For Augustine's ridicule of the Manichaean specialists' promises to be rational (*pollicitator[es] rationis*)—in this instance, about trees with souls—see Augustine, *mor.* 2.17.55.
[26] Jason David BeDuhn, *Augustine's Manichaean Dilemma: Making a "Catholic" Self, 388–401 C.E.* (Philadelphia: University of Pennsylvania Press, 2013), 204–5.

Augustine of his time with the Manichees? Perhaps, yet he was aware that his polemical purposes in the anti-Manichaean initiatives were as well served by concentrating on his adversaries' boasting as by drilling into their doctrine. He never tired of reprimanding them for being so taken with their own presumed celebrity. By contrast, Augustine pointed out, the churches' leaders disliked public display and were uninterested in fame.[27] Their reserve, he said, made them worthy disciples of Jesus, whereas the Manichaean specialists seemed to have fashioned their arrogance to match the boasting of their pretentious founder, the third-century Persian prophet Mani, who was heard by critics proclaiming himself the Paraclete.[28] Augustine may have read or only heard about his declaration, but we know he implied that the sect's elite pulled a similar stunt, bragging about its special affinity with the divine to give its doctrines greater weight.[29]

The arrogance was apparent to him before he left Italy, and he confided, while still among the Manichees, that he suspected the sect's specialists of using their reputations for superior righteousness to amass wealth and seduce women. Yet he admitted that rumors of salacious conduct and self-indulgence may have distorted the reality they professed to register.[30] Indeed, much of his information about the Manichees' misconduct was secondhand, for cultic activities were not among his chief concerns until he converted to Christianity. But, by the late fourth century, he had become good at deploying what he learned to the Manichaean specialists' disadvantage. He turned their diet into a scandal, trading effectively on the conceit that the elite consecrated and purified food by consuming it. That notion, Augustine explained, justified the specialists' eating to excess and leaving nothing for their famished servers; the elite, he said, lavished greater care on cucumbers than on its corps of attendants.[31]

---

[27] Augustine, *util. cred.* 2.4.
[28] Reported in Hegemonius, *Acta Archelai* (Louvain: Brepols, 2001), 27.3.
[29] Augustine, *conf.* 3.10.6: *dicebant: "veritas et veritas, et multum eam dicebant mihi, et nusquam erat in eis.... [Q]ualibus ego tunc pascebar inanibus et non pascebar.*
[30] Augustine, *mor.* 2.19.68.
[31] Augustine, *mor.* 2.16.52-53: *magis cucumerem quam hominem miseraris*. For the relative unimportance of cultic practices to Augustine during his association with the sect, consult Jason David BeDuhn, *Augustine's Manichaean Dilemma: Conversion and Apostasy, 373–388 C.E.* (Philadelphia: University of Pennsylvania Press, 2010), 163–64.

The specialists' claims about their superior righteousness and virtuosity seemed to him nothing more than cover for their misanthropy. And he looked to ridicule the cosmology behind and bracing those claims. He sifted their stories about the entrapment of light in creation by a prince of darkness and about the constant conflict between darkness and light.[32] The specialists encouraged and capitalized on their followers' belief that only the sect's elite could liberate the light. Admiring auditors placed their homes and daughters at the specialists' disposal, so they could inscribe themselves in the enterprise of emancipation. Meanwhile, the sect's elite lived parasitically—thoughtlessly and uselessly (*tam vana et inepta*).[33] Dismantling the displays of specialists' self-righteousness and ordinary Manichees' uncritical devotion could well have started Augustine thinking censoriously about self-reliance as well as about boasting, and he continued his efforts to undermine both as he approached the powerful but especially as he reproached Pelagians.

Powerful officials, he explained to one of them—Vicar Macedonius—were likely to misinterpret the church's efforts to assist them. He had written to urge clemency for persons whose criminal activity had been directed against Catholic Christians, but apparently the vicar had bristled; he did not appreciate a prelate interrupting court procedures in mid-gallop. Gingerly, Augustine suggested that politically responsible individuals, however astute they might be, went off course in the home stretch occasionally when they relied on their own powers of discernment and neglected prelates' offers to be of use.[34] Macedonius was hardly boasting, yet he did assume the government could do very well without the church's interference. As for the Pelagians' self-reliance, it had come to Augustine's attention as admirers of Pelagius came from Italy to Africa during the second decade of the fifth century. They seemed to him to be attributing to the faithful the lion's share of the work in, and the credit for, their salvation. The gravity of the problem was obvious to Augustine. He kept cramming unsolicited warnings against this new "heresy" into his exegetical remarks, which

---

[32]Augustine, *c. Sec.* 2.19.2.
[33]Augustine, *c. Faust.* 5.10.
[34]Augustine, ep. 155.5. For the vicar's original response to the church's overture, see Augustine, ep. 152.2.

recycled and amplified the objections he had registered in previous anti-Manichaean treatises and in sermons he preached soon after becoming bishop.[35] Preaching on the apostle Paul's injunction against boasting, for example, he explained that Christians only properly understood the source, application, and purpose of the virtues they possessed once they had conceded their inability to develop or deploy them unaided by God. The faithful, he insisted, ought to hold firm what they were given without boasting about their gifts: *datum tene, sed datorem agnosce*.[36]

In those earliest sermons, the principal braggarts, aside from the Manichaean elite were Jews who purportedly claimed to possess the power to obey God's laws revealed in their sacred texts. Augustine argued that they greatly underestimated their susceptibility to temptation. They believed they were sufficiently robust to resist, but their souls were too sick, he said, to come up with a cure.[37] After 410, Augustine figured he found new Jews among the Pelagians whose theorists trusted humans to embrace Christianity and persevere in the faith without God's special, persistent assistance.[38] Their boasting to that effect stirred him to emphasize the priority of God's grace and to deny prevenient virtuous behavior had any influence whatsoever on its presence or persistence in the faithful. Predestination ought to be preached, he urged, to offset the appeal of the Pelagians' meritocratic frame of reference. To be sure, grace was the cure; only God could administer it, although sermons stressing predestination prepared patients to receive it and to express gratitude rather than gall.[39]

Caelestius, who had arrived in North Africa by 411, seems to have been the first Pelagian to upset prelates there. Augustine promptly wrote against his faith in human nature, which, if we may judge from the bishop's rebuttal, was partly based on texts that praised biblical protagonists for their probity. God was

---

[35]See, for example, Augustine, *retr.* 2.36 and Augustine, ep. 140.85.
[36]Augustine, s. 160.2, citing 1 Cor. 1.31 and 4.7.
[37]Augustine, s. 160.7: *numquam se sanat aegrotus*.
[38]Augustine, s. 131.10: *quod ergo dictum est de Judaeis, hoc omnino in istis videmus*.
[39]Augustine, *persev.* 21.54: *praedestinatio praedicanda est*. Pierre-Marie Hombert, *Gloria Gratiae: Se glorifier en Dieu, principe et fin de la théologie augustinienne de la grâce* (Paris: Institut d'Études Augustiniennes, 1996), 333–34 classifies such sermons as "medicinal."

reported to have called Job blameless, but, Augustine counseled, one should not infer that Job or any other mortal was—or ever could be—sinless.⁴⁰ Still, Augustine's reply to Caelestius seems reserved to Marie-François Berrouard, who suspects that the bishop was finding it hard at the time to integrate the apostle Paul's graphically described ambivalence ("I see in my members another law . . . making me captive to . . . sin") with a doctrine of divine sovereignty and predestination. Berrouard suggests Augustine was mindful that Pelagians were poised to pounce, should he concede any effectiveness to Paul struggling to suppress that "law" and breaking his captivity to sin.⁴¹ Nonetheless, before one early anti-Pelagian treatise finished, Augustine had confidently pit humans' self-satisfaction with righteousness achieved against God's unmerited intervention and righteousness granted. So there was no cause for gloating: struggles and ultimate victories were prescribed, choreographed, and won by God.⁴²

Pelagians were interested in striving for righteousness and the merit purportedly attached to it. From the start of his ministry, Augustine discouraged a different sort of striving, as we have heard and will hear again; in one of his earliest sermons, before becoming bishop, he frowned on the seemingly surging and insatiable thirst for political status and influence, which reinforced the exaggerated self-esteem or boasting that kept Christians captive to sin and—later, for Agamben—would keep citizens captive to sovereign powers. Augustine advised Christians to forsake the witch's brew of greed and glory and to look forward to the expanse of eternity. And the joy they would find in faith that God had reserved a place for them in that hereafter, he added, was greater than the pleasures they might take here and now in moral or material advantages tempting them to boast.⁴³

Julian of Eclanum, who became one of Pelagianism's most prolific defenders, suggested that Augustine's complaints about boasting

---

⁴⁰Augustine, *pecc. mer.* 2.12.17–2.13.18, discussing Job 1:8.
⁴¹Marie-François Berrouard, "L'exégèse augustinienne de Rom. 7.7-25 entre 396 et 418," *Recherches augustiniennes* 16 (1981), 143–44, citing Rom. 7.19-23.
⁴²Augustine, *pecc. mer.* 2.34.55: *statuit Deus, ut post ejus peccatum propagata caro peccati ad recipiendam justitiam laboribus et molestiis niteretur.*
⁴³Augustine, s. 260c.7; Augustine, *en. Ps.* 67.4.

thinly camouflaged self-loathing at the center of his theology. Julian accused him of ladling Manichaean dualisms into emerging Catholic Christian orthodoxy. Was Augustine so concerned with arrogance that he would make all humans vile and turn the self into a prison for the soul? Augustine answered, clarifying that sin within was not an active agent, as the Manichees had suggested, but a deficiency. Humanity's struggles with sinful impulses—struggles that the apostle Paul vividly presented—ideally taught the faithful to finish fussing about the gain or loss of worldly pleasures and glory and to intensify their hope, braced by faith, to acquire everlasting, celestial joy. Augustine reminded Julian that Jesus promised as much. So the same God who created humanity's first parents without defects and presided over the creation of their defective descendants redeemed the faithful, because they embraced Jesus's promise and exhibited their hopes in love for others and by glorifying God instead of extolling and ennobling their own efforts.[44]

Augustine, at the time, was also troubled by Christians who, to his mind, insufficiently honored Jesus by criticizing the Christology formulated at the Council of Nicaea. Anti-Nicene Christians objected to the ostensible elevation of Jesus. The early fourth-century council hoisted the son of God up to God, making him equal to and consubstantial with the Father. Augustine's endorsement was bundled with his complaints about Pelagians. He said Christianity had no room for anyone undecided about—or dissenting from—the faith's fundamental premise, that the Word of God in the womb of his mother was indissolubly bound to human nature, and the way he phrased it—emphasizing an absence of preceding merit (*sine ullis praecentibus bonorum operum meritis*)—suggests that he tugged Pelagians into the quarrel.[45]

Elsewhere, Augustine economized as well, striking simultaneously at Pelagian and anti-Nicene theorists. Father and Son were equal, he declared, yet Jesus, by no means inferior, never boasted. He was God's son "by generation" yet unhesitatingly glorified his Father. The faithful, still fettered to the flesh, however, could only hope to become sons by adoption, but they were prone to boast.[46]

---

[44] Augustine, *c. Iul. imp.* 6.14.
[45] Augustine, *trin.* 15.26.46.
[46] Augustine, *en. Ps.* 50.19, citing Rom. 8:23-25; Augustine, *Io. ev. tr.* 35.4.

Hence, it seems no exaggeration to say, as Pierre-Marie Hombert does, that the deflation of inflated egos was one of Augustine's constant preoccupations. After he encountered what he took to be the Pelagians' reconstruction of Christianity as moral philosophy, Augustine underscored the distinctions between human nature and its powers, on one hand, and God's power and saving presence, on the other.[47]

After 410, that is, Augustine repeatedly scolded the Pelagians for presuming that the very existence of biblical laws and "oughts" proved that humanity—unassisted by grace, other than the grace received in baptism—was fit to obey and oblige, respectively. Had proponents of emerging orthodoxy who complained of their confidence so embittered them that they refused to see how impaired human nature was? Did they frame exaggerated claims about moral enterprise to cater to patrons who aspired to be independent (and deserving)? Much of Augustine's *City of God*, which he started to write shortly after Pelagians and their treatises landed in Africa, could be taken as commentary on comparable desires to control one's destiny.

What historian Peter Brown, attributing this view to Augustine, describes as "an omnipotent denial of dependence" was the defining feature of the personal and political endeavors in what the *City* describes as "this wicked world," through which the faithful sojourn as pilgrims. Brown holds that Augustine "demolished" "with exceptional savagery" the pagans' and Pelagians' ethical theories. The latter appeared to him to inspire arrogance, the obstacle to giving God due credit; the former credited their deities as well as the heroes of their empire and republic for giving free rein to their lust for domination. Augustine strenuously objected, and he grew evermore eager to explain what was wrong with Rome.[48]

---

[47]See the letter Augustine, Alypius, Aurelius of Carthage, and several other African bishops sent to Rome in 416; Augustine, ep. 177.2-11. Also see Hombert, *Gloria Gratiae*, 463: *préoccupation toujour présente ... eviter que homme ne s'enorgueillisse*.
[48]For the lust for domination in "this wicked world" (*in hoc saeculo maligno*), see Augustine, *civ*. 1.30, 3.14, 14.5, and 18.49 and what follows in the next section of this chapter. For Peter Brown's observations, see his *Augustine of Hippo*, 326–29.

What's wrong with Rome?

Prosperity. Emissaries from the past—notably, Sallust, Varro, Livy, and Cicero— helped Augustine make the case that public morality declined soon after the progenitors of the republic eliminated the last of the city's kings. Augustine echoed Sallust's assessment that fear forced Romans to put the interests of the city and its territories before their own during the wars with Carthaginians in the third century BCE. Soon after the enemy's defeat and the destruction of Carthage, however, Romans forgot the exhilaration that attended city solidarity, recycled their corrupt practices, and left Rome in a disgraceful state.[49] Public authorities protected prerogatives of the most affluent and influential citizens. They and others were more concerned with increase than integrity. Speeches about Rome's glory and leading citizens' nobility—eulogies presumably similar to those Augustine gave in Milan when he was politically ambitious—constituted part of the plutocrats' concerted effort to mollify their inferiors. They were stocked with pretty fictions, Augustine said, to keep citizens in awe of the commercial and political elites. Romans had been ruled—and Rome ruled—more justly at some times than at others, he granted, without specifying the better times or arrangements prior to Constantine's conversion. But, referring to politics in the African provinces in the early fifth century, he echoed Cicero's lament: customs that made for a righteous political culture seemed to be all but forgotten (*oblivione obsoletos*) and certainly not cherished by politicians or patent in their proceedings. Prosperity and pleasure kept elites arrogant and unaware of or indifferent to their corruption and that of their political retainers.[50]

The trick, as noted, was to keep inferiors from listening to and learning from critics who cared more for morality than for material prosperity. Officials' task, as Robert Dodaro concisely summarized Augustine's account of it—which corresponds with Agamben's complaints about a technically proficient yet overbearing set of sovereign powers' protocols and spectacles—was to "encod[e] the

---

[49] Augustine, *civ.* 2.18: *colluvie morum pessimorum quo illa civitas prolapsa fuerit.*
[50] Augustine, *civ.* 2.21, citing Cicero's *De Re Publica* 5.1.

principles of an obsequious clientism" attractively.[51] But the appetite for glory was such that the powerful also demanded respect from their clients, Augustine confirmed, pondering his *City*'s chapters on Rome's decline. To get respect they were ready to sponsor games catering to clients' wickedly inordinate desires (*ludicra malae cupiditatis*).[52] Leading citizens were gratified as long as their inferiors were *subditi*, more subjects than citizens, and more objects than subjects. For their part, inferiors were content, Augustine went on, as long as their patrons tolerated indiscretions and indolence among the proles. This nasty, unspoken agreement between the powers that be and commoners seemed responsible for making life in the capital a cesspool but also for polluting the African provinces. Provincial executives, Augustine said, were prized as long as they had no passion for probity (*non . . . rector[es] morum*) and were concerned only for powerful constituents' safety and luxury. It looked as if proconsuls' and proconsular legates' *raison d'être* was simply to oppose disturbers of the peace and of class privilege. So, Augustine added wryly, all that would be required of their gods was that they keep enemies and plagues at bay while keeping the true state of their states under wraps. And if the Romans and provincials were fortunate to have officials who could do just that and no more, Augustine guessed the citizens would not hesitate to make them gods.[53]

A few fortunate pagan officials enjoyed success, but the gods failed miserably; neither the republic nor the empire went unmolested for long stretches. The pagans' claim that Roman history only took a turn for the worse after Constantine and several of his successors converted, vandalizing the gods' temples to make churches, was false and malicious, Augustine argued; his rejoinder, as we shall see, was his *City of God*'s first ten books. But he also defended Christian emperors in a letter to Marcellinus while he contemplated the trajectory of his answer to pagans. There, and in the *City*, he borrowed from Sallust to blame prosperity for misrule

---

[51] Robert Dodaro, "Eloquent Lies, Just Wars, and the Politics of Persuasion: Reading Augustine's *City of God* in a Postmodern World," *Augustinian Studies* 25 (1994), 83.
[52] Augustine, s. 32.20.
[53] Augustine, *civ*. 2.20.

and for the pandemic of ambition and envy we heard him lament in the previous chapter.[54]

Sallust had conceded that conflict was the very stuff of republican Rome's politics. Animosities were manageable, until prosperity tempted the patricians to be shamefully self-indulgent at the expense of plebeians—and, in turn, prompted plebeians recklessly to take to extremes their efforts to have grievances addressed. In his *City of God* Augustine described how license and luxury unsettled Rome centuries before his faith—and his God unseated pagans' gods. He labored his claim that pagan nostalgia for regimes preserved by their gods was absurd. The regimes were usually ruthless; officials' and citizens' behavior was reprehensible. Did pagans' deities suppose that moral supervision was beyond their remit? How could Romans read their republic's and empire's history and miss "the fact" that, on their gods' watch, sedition and cynicism—not civic piety—was the rule, leading to civil wars that had been barbarously waged and even more barbarously concluded?[55]

Augustine may have singled out Caius Marius for special mention because he had been an enemy of Africans even before Numidia became a Roman province. And Marius was adept, hectoring friends and foes alike and stirring civil unrest. He was known to have been especially savage suppressing insurgents, according to Sallust, who had Marius leave Africa littered with corpses and athrob with mourning (*luctu atque caede*).[56] Marius's campaigns occurred more than five hundred years before Augustine became bishop, but he figured Marius would prove a sensational specimen, an example of how the pagans' gods rewarded brutality, for Marius had been elected consul seven times, despite or because

---

[54]Augustine, ep. 138.16.
[55]Augustine, *civ.* 2.22: *ut in bella etiam progrederentur civilia causis iniquissimis suscepta et crudeliter gesta crudeliusque finita.* For critics' attacks on prodigality that linked financial and moral devastation, consult Catherine Edwards, *The Politics of Immorality in Ancient Rome* (Cambridge; Cambridge University Press, 2002), 173–206; for "the healthful antagonism of Sallust's republic" and connections between conflict and injustice, see Daniel Kapust, *Republicanism, Rhetoric, and Roman Political Thought* (Cambridge: Cambridge University Press, 2011), 43–52.
[56]Sall. *Iug.* 92.4.

of his cruelty. *Ita Mario cuncta procedere*, Sallust said; everything fell Marius's way.[57]

Augustine translated this as bloodied luck (*sanguineam felicitatem*). Had the gods been unlucky or did they turn a blind eye to Marius's various crimes? The pagans' historians simply recorded them, leaving Augustine to exploit the report, indict the deities, and question whether paganism could ever thereafter refer to their gods as upright, vigilant overseers. That Marius's depravity was so well rewarded—his seventh consulship was unprecedented—discredited any proclamation to that effect and, Augustine believed, ought to choke off pagans' nostalgia for the peace and civic righteousness over which their gods presumably presided before the coming of Christianity. Marius's wealth, health, honors, and longevity ought to give pagans pause before connecting Rome's glory, Romans' personal glory, and their gods' powers, leaving Christianity and its God responsible for what he allowed were sad and difficult times.[58]

Many pagans continued to boast. They refused to think their deities vacated in favor of the Christians' God. They congratulated themselves on answered prayers for changes in weather or for the survival of some cults. But nothing should be inferred from rainfall when rain is asked of the gods, Augustine answered; temporal benefits had absolutely no bearing on matters of much greater significance between creatures and their creator.[59] The contrary assumption might have haunted Augustine, as Franz Georg Maier suggests, inasmuch as one of his patrons, the Roman prefect Quintus Aurelius Symmachus, repeatedly petitioned emperors during the 380s to restore the Altar of Victory to the Senate. It commemorated the victory at Actium that enabled Octavian Caesar to become Augustus, the first Roman emperor. The implication of restoration would have been clear to pagans: that the gods were present and powerful at the time (29 BCE), awaited an opportunity to make a comeback, and could be counted on to restore the empire's glory once the Christians' God was more widely cursed for having made a mess.[60]

---

[57] Sall. *Iug.* 65.5.
[58] Augustine, *civ.* 2.23.
[59] Augustine, *en. Ps.* 98.14.
[60] Franz Georg Maier, *Augustin und das antike Rom* (Stuttgart: Kohlhammer, 1955), 119–20.

Augustine had yet to commit to Christianity and clerical office when Symmachus asked and was denied, yet it is easy to imagine the near miss concerned him as he deposited Marius in his *City* and added other evidence of the pagan gods' inattentiveness. The story of Saguntum was perfect for his purpose. Relationships between Rome and the Saguntines on the southern coast of the Iberian Peninsula are hard to define. We know Saguntum requested and received a delegation from Rome in the 220s BCE. Apparently the Romans were trusted to referee a disagreement in the city and propose an armistice of sorts. When the Carthaginian commander Hannibal besieged Saguntum in 219, attempting to reassert Carthage's influence in those parts of its Iberian empire left after the First Punic War, the Saguntines again appealed to Rome. Historian John Lazenby stigmatizes the response as "lethargic." Rome offered no help during the siege and declared war on Carthage only after the Saguntines' city had been sacked.[61] But what Lazenby calls "lethargy," Augustine characterized as "shabby and shameful." While Hannibal lay siege, Romans dispatched envoys, not troops. Livy, Augustine's likely source, left no doubt that the Saguntines, as Rome's allies, deserved better—soldiers rather than diplomats.[62] Diplomacy got nowhere, and Hannibal refused to lift the siege. Conditions within the city worsened. Augustine's censure is unsparing. The account in his *City* proceeds quickly from siege to famine to slaughter and Saguntum's destruction.[63]

Augustine failed to mention (as Livy did not) that opposition to Hannibal and to his Iberian initiative was surfacing in Carthage, where war-weary citizens warned that the Saguntum siege would lock them into a conflict with Rome, too soon after Rome had taken Sicily, Sardinia, and Corsica from them.[64] Augustine preferred to omit factors that could well have given Romans reasons to negotiate. Plausibly, Hannibal's critics at home, given time, might have forced him to retreat. The results of sending Saguntines reinforcements

---

[61]John F. Lazenby, "Rome and Carthage," in *The Cambridge Companion to the Roman Republic*, ed. Harriet Flower (Cambridge: Cambridge University Press, 2014), 266.
[62]Livy, *Ab urbe condita* 21.6.3-4.
[63]Augustine, *civ.* 3.20: *Dum hae morae aguntur, misera illa civitas opulentissima suae rei publicae Romanaeque carissima, octavo vel nono a Poenis mense delata est.*
[64]Livy, *Ab urbe condita* 21.10.10.

would almost certainly have included Roman casualties, at the very least, and, far more unpleasant, another gargantuan, costly clash between the two Mediterranean empires. But Augustine was not out to exonerate the Romans. Saguntum, seen as a betrayal, gave him too tempting a chance to censure the Romans' gods for having refused to inspire aggressive intervention. The Saguntines—also pagans, but generally forgotten in the fifth century—came off better in Augustine's *City*. Their fidelity to Rome was more important to him than Hannibal's villainy. Their loyalty helped Augustine score a second point against the Romans' gods. Saguntum had a choice, he recalled; they could remain Rome's allies and risk their safety—which they did—or capitulate to the Carthaginians and save their city. Pagan deities presided over that choice, Augustine sneered, unfavorably comparing the sway or regime of pagans gods, as his contemporaries and critics reconstructed it, with the supervision or sovereignty of the Christians' God who presided over a cosmos in which security, salvation, and fidelity were parts of a single, comprehensive, celestial strategy in which the pilgrim city of God on earth can only be safely—and the celestial city everlastingly—possessed by faith.[65]

Augustine's pagan critics could have replied that Rome had been spared when Hannibal, after the sack of Saguntum, crossed the Alps into Italy and campaigned there with some notable successes for fifteen years. Symmachus was sure that Romans' devotion to their cults and gods was responsible not only for the outcome at Actium and for the battlefield successes thereafter but for the capital's survival during Hannibal's descent into Italy.[66] Augustine's *City*, finishing its narrative of the Saguntines' fidelity and fate, however, turned the argument from material security to integrity. Romans and their gods had abandoned the Saguntines, their steadfast Spanish friends, to their terrible fate. Where was the glory in that?[67]

---

[65] Augustine, *civ.* 22.6: *Profecto enim Saguntini si salutem eligerent, fides eis fuerat deserenda; si fides tenenda, amittenda utique salus, sicut factum est. . . . Salus autem civitatis Dei talis est, ut cum fide ac per fidem teneri vel potius adquiri possit.*

[66] Symmachus, *Relatio* 3.9: *Hic cultus in leges meas orbem redegit, haec sacra Hannibalem a moenibus . . . reppulerunt.* Also see Giovanni Brizzi, *Canne: La sconfitta che fece vincere Roma* (Bologna: Mulino, 2016), 43–55, 136–43 and Jakob Seibert, *Forschungen zu Hannibal* (Darmstadt: Wissenschaftliche Buchgesellschaft, 1993), 217–41.

[67] Augustine, *civ.* 3.20.

The argument that devotion to Rome's old cults and the glory of republican and early imperial Rome were closely connected as cause and effect made no sense to Augustine. After having chronicled the gods' indulgence of Caius Marius and apparent indifference to Rome's desertion of Saguntum, he may have hoped that thoughtful pagans would question the equation of religious piety and patriotism. Yet he read how readily Rome's heroes sacrificed their lives to display its civic and military ideals. Their stories were popular among the pagans whom he was trying to impress with his *City*'s contrast between Christian and pagan fortitude.[68] But Augustine had stories, too, in addition to those of Marius's treachery and the betrayal of Saguntum. He liked cataloging the civil wars that nearly wrecked the late republic and relished rehearsing the career of one would-be consul who, Sallust and Cicero had convinced him, would have destroyed it.[69]

In 63 BCE, the last attempt of Lucius Sergius Catilina to be elected consul failed. He then persuaded disaffected aristocrats to plot against the Roman Senate and against Cicero, who had engineered Catiline's final electoral defeat. To attract commoners to the conspirators' cause, Catiline promised tax relief. He vowed to free Romans from debt and, in one oration that Sallust included in his account, he pledged to restore Rome's glory. Sallust's Catiline knew just how to appeal to the multitude.[70] And thanks to Sallust's and Cicero's tales of the disturbances that his appeals occasioned, few citizens thereafter would have stared uncomprehendingly when Catiline was introduced into their conversations. But the aspiring consul and conspirator had only cameo roles in Augustine's early works. At Cassiciacum, Trygetius, one of the interlocutors, insinuated Catiline into his proof that virtues—in this instance, Cicero's—were in evidence without dramatic display: disclosing the conspiracy and Catiline's dark side, Cicero discreetly exhibited prudence, temperance, fortitude, and justice. Augustine thought both the anecdote and assessment worth recording in his *De ordine*.[71]

---

[68] Augustine, *civ.* 5.18.
[69] Augustine, *civ.* 3.30.
[70] Sall. *Cat.* 20.14: *Quin igitur expergiscimini? En illa quam saepe optastis libertas, praeterea divitiae, decus, gloria in oculis sita sunt.*
[71] Augustine, *ord.* 2.7.22.

Catiline's other appearances in Augustine's early work were also brief and relatively casual. Sifting motives for illicit behavior, he mentioned Catiline in his *Confessions*, but the seriousness of the conflicts centuries before seemed less germane to the topic than Augustine's own larceny in his youth.[72] Censuring Manichaean specialists' misconduct, he inserted Catiline to illustrate villainy and hypocrisy not unlike theirs, but the comparison went nowhere.[73] When Augustine began writing his *City*, however, he called on Catiline to undermine pagan confidence that their gods and Romans' glory were closely linked. Catiline's run had been inglorious, to say the least; had his conspiracy run its course, Augustine speculated, the rebellion would have done far greater damage than what the Goths did on entering Rome in the early fifth century. Catiline had been a homegrown criminal yet more barbarous than the empire's subsequent enemies from beyond the pale. Recycling what he learned from his sources, Augustine referred to Catiline and his accomplices as parricides; they were prepared to fire up factions, create crevices, and then leave Rome in ruins, if the Senate refused to appease them.[74]

Augustine probably was too taken with his tyrant's striking belligerence, treachery, and brutality to consider what might pass as a strong counterargument. For Catiline's failure, on the gods' watch, preserved the capital and its cults. Caius Marius and Catiline, consul and would-be consul, were paired because, also on the gods' watch, they successfully drew others into their orbits, cloaking sinister intents with their praise for—and promises to restore—Rome's glory. Outcomes mattered when Marius took center stage, inasmuch as he had succeeded, whereas Catiline failed miserably; his revolt was on life support when he died in battle, clutching a memento of Marius.[75]

Pagans' gods got no credit in Augustine's *City* for Catiline's failure. The narrative makes them doubly culpable: they allowed Catiline to attract scoundrels and revel in the possibility of

---

[72] Augustine, *conf.* 2.5.11.
[73] Augustine, *mor.* 2.13.28.
[74] Augustine, *civ.* 1.5–1.7: *Sed hi videlicet perditi et patriae parricidae* (1.5). See Cic. *Cat.* 4.6.14, for a similar prophesy (*totam Italiam vastandam diripiendamque*).
[75] Augustine, *civ.* 2.23. Sall. *Cat.* 59.3 mentions the memento.

overturning the political order, and they allowed the capital to fall into such a sordid state that ordinary citizens were also charmed by him and joined the dissolute and profligate in his ranks.[76] Augustine approached his sources, Cicero and Sallust, with warrants for search and seizure, and he came away with the motley, sinister crew, whom they excoriated. Catiline's popularity, even though it ebbed, supposedly showed pagans' faith was flawed and foolish. Their gods were unreal and untrustworthy; Augustine, as narrator, could have it both ways—and did.[77]

In another text, his extended response to Julian of Eclanum, he seems kinder to Catiline. Revisiting the conspiracy, he suggests that the would-be consul's appeal to Rome's former glory was stirring. Moreover, his accomplices' solidarity along with his broad, albeit temporary, appeal attested his sincerity, if not his virtue. At the time one might have mistaken Catiline's persistence for fortitude, yet Augustine was ready with a disclaimer: in the conspiracy's aftermath only dullards could come to such conclusions (*Quis haec sapiat nisi desipiat*). Even a relatively creditable Roman virtue—fortitude or courage—turns ugly, he claimed, as a single shade and not part of a palate of virtues. To the extent that virtues served Rome's glory well, they did so in an ensemble, and, serving Rome's glory rather than God's, any virtue or any palate of virtues, in Augustine's estimation, loses all its luster.[78]

Franz Georg Maier's trenchant analysis of Augustine's remarks on Romans' virtues and Roman glory still rewards careful reading. It reminds us of Augustine's conviction that, as long as civic virtues were prized and practiced to gain and enhance personal or political reputations, their purpose discredited their pursuit. When glory comes to be measured in material, political, or psychological terms and becomes virtues' *raison d'être*, the virtues are far less virtuous *sub specie aeternitatis*.[79] Augustine's *City* is quite emphatic

---

[76] Augustine, *civ.* 3.2.
[77] Augustine, ep. 167.7. For the aristocratic bias that drew Augustine to his sources and likely encouraged him to connect Catiline's charisma with commoners' credulity, see Claire Sotinel, "Le personnel épiscopal: Enquête sur la puissance de l'évêque dans la cité," *L'Évêque dans la cité du IVe au Ve siècle: Image et autorité*, ed. Sotinel and Éric Rebillard (Rome: École Française de Rome, 1998), 124.
[78] Augustine, *c. Iul.* 4.3.19.
[79] Maier, *Augustin und das antike Rom*, 129.

on that count, insisting that authentic virtue is directed to a good immeasurably better than any material, political, or psychological advantage. Genuine virtues glorify God and inspire the faithful to pay forward God's love for creation in their love for others.[80]

Augustine made no secret of his dislike for glory hounds hustling after glory, as the world understands it—and for historians who touted the virtue of doing so. He reminded Christians that Jesus instructed the apostles not to be good to gain acclaim. They were, in one respect, to be like Roman heroes who exhibited courage and fortitude as a duty to their *patria*. But the faithful had a *patria* quite different from the one that inspired pagans to sacrifice ritually and inspirationally on battlefields. As pilgrims, the faithful were to sacrifice or surrender their pursuits of material advantage and reputation. They were to cultivate virtues that reflected their *patria*, a celestial homeland. The apostles had introduced into their missions and ministries a sense of self-transcendence that went well beyond the heroism of celebrated consuls and commanders, sacrificing to serve Rome, whose celebrity was their immortality. The immortality that evangelists and apostles were promised was celestial and everlasting.[81]

In Augustine's *City*, discussions of the exertions of Rome's heroes and of Christianity's apostles and martyrs were, after a fashion, revisionist history lessons well suited to the text. To Christians who were less intrepid than their faith's founders and early missionaries, a different pitch was appropriate. Without specific examples, Augustine tried to make ordinary Christians conscious of the stranglehold the world's sense of glory had on their ambitions, so he preached against lavishing attention and affection on what this world loves and respects. The faithful were faced with torrents of temptations to be liked and admired, he acknowledged, yet succumbing to them risked more than what might immediately be perceived. They must draw away from what the world loves, as consistently as their faith's heroes did when the consequences of opposition to sovereign powers were lethal.[82] For Christians who come to love praise inordinately cannot love truth, glorify God, and

---

[80] Augustine, *civ.* 5.12.
[81] Augustine, *civ.* 5.14.
[82] Augustine, *Io. ev. tr.* 87.4.

pay God's love forward, Augustine told them, inasmuch as all three required a degree of estrangement and detachment from protocols and values of this world.[83] He did not claim those values and the virtues that showcased them were totally useless. At their best, virtues associated with personal and political glory bridled impulses that, left unchecked, ensured that creatures' war on vice would end badly. Concern for one's name or fame—selfish as it might seem—could counter the persistent tug of one's basest instincts. Frowning on citizens' self-assertion, Augustine nonetheless could not deny that citizens' desires to call attention to their civic pride resulted in improved public works. The pursuit of personal glory in public service sometimes acted as a brake against disgraceful and socially disruptive behavior.[84]

Might statements of this sort qualify as approval of the pagans' virtues? Robert Dodaro appropriately objects to that characterization, reminding us that neither Augustine's *City* nor his sermons were anything but skeptical about the Romans' love of praise. It promoted flattery to a privileged position and kept some boasting and many cowering. At best, it was a fault, useful—though not admirable.[85] Despite superficial resemblances, Christians' virtues—informed by an otherworldly trajectory for glory—were very different from those of their pagan neighbors. The Christians' virtues were propelled by a faith that God set the course for them and set them on it. Practicing virtue on that course, they discovered how different their faith, hope, and loves were from those of self-assertive others.[86]

Neither those others nor the gods whom they worshipped and on whom they counted, Augustine argued, did a good job glorifying Rome. To him, Caius Marius, Catiline, and Rome's betrayal of the Saguntines proved precisely that. As Pierre-Marie Hombert points out, Augustine finally let the gods out of the dock and rained blame down on pagans who had been and still were devoted to them. He

---

[83]Augustine, *civ.* 5.13-14.
[84]Augustine, *civ.* 19.4.
[85]See Dodaro, *Christ and the Just Society*, 183–84 and Jennifer Herdt, "The Theater of the Virtues: Augustine's Critique of Pagan Mimesis," in *Augustine's "City of God": A Critical Guide*, ed. James Wetzel (Cambridge: Cambridge University Press, 2012), 125–28.
[86]Augustine, *civ.* 18.54; Augustine, *en. Ps.* 118(5).4.

mocked their fixation on glory, a preoccupation for which Rome's poets were particularly culpable.[87] As for Christians, Augustine's sermons left them with a clear choice. To want to be praised and admired was comprehensible to him, but it would make them uneasy, he said, insofar as, cherishing the esteem of others more than God's love and approval, they would be as adulterers awaiting Jesus to come and judge their choices, as adulterers living in fear that their spouses would arrive home at an inopportune time.[88]

Augustine, the preacher, could be strident opposing popularity to piety and comparing a passion for praise to adultery, but Augustine, the historian, appears to have been more forgiving. His *City* supposes that God surrendered Romans the territory they conquered on the grounds that their love of praise and glory led them to trade their safety for the security of their subjects. God foreknew Rome's rulers would see public service as a path to glory and praise. So God conferred an empire on them because, in effect, they smothered some faults with others.[89] Augustine, as we learned, figured that the Romans' love of praise kept them relatively honest. That love was still a fault, yet, as Rome expanded, no Christian preachers were there to compare pagans' love or lust for others' praise with adultery. Christianity came precisely to that conclusion, but Augustine was still willing to compliment Romans' virtuosity, which brought order, roads, and a measure of peace to the Mediterranean world. Yet the *City*'s historian could not stop preaching for long. For all the Romans did, suppressed, and suffered for their republic's and empire's enlargement, security, and glory, he said, should put in perspective what Christians should be ready to suffer and suppress for a greater cause and reward, for the glory of God and for their place—and their peace—in the celestial city.[90]

---

[87] Hombert, *Gloria Gratiae*, 228.
[88] Augustine, *en. Ps.* 118(12).3.
[89] Augustine, *civ.* 5.13: *voluit Deus et occidentale fieri . . . imperii latitudine et magnitudine illustrius, idque talibus potissimum concessit hominibus ad domanda gravia mala multarum gentium, qui causa honoris laudis et gloriae consuluerunt patriae, in qua ipsam gloriam requirebant, salutemque eius saluti suae praeponere non dubitaverunt, pro isto uno vitio, id est amore laudis, pecuniae cupiditatem et multa alia vitia comprimentes.*
[90] Augustine, *civ.* 5.17.

The contrast was sharper still as Augustine reflected on the indomitable lust for domination that developed from the Romans' love of praise. Chances are that he was also thinking about the ambition and envy which, as we learned, he associated with the pagans' political culture. Come Christianity—and Augustine—the exaggerated self-esteem that allegedly fueled their desire to dominate seemed irrational as the western empire contracted. Nonetheless, the *City* supposes that nothing was done in history without God's authorization, so the Romans' lust, their territorial expanse, and their losses were predetermined. That did not make the lust to dominate any less offensive to Augustine. It robbed statesmen of their dignity, he said, and put them in the company of thieves. He recycled an old tale to make the point. The *City* recounts a conversation between Alexander the Great and a pirate he captured. The former asked why his pirate-prisoner had taken to a life of larceny. His answer, dipped in insolence: there is little to choose between what the great Alexander and the pirate did, save that history refers to it as an empire and conquest when done with a fleet and as piracy when done with a single ship.[91] The comparison criminalized the lust to dominate, as, one suspects, was Augustine's intent, though God had allowed rule to pass from Babylon to Rome, from one empire to another. Augustine's judgment, nonetheless, was unfavorable, to say the least. Rome's decadence showed. Leading, bragging citizens' love for praise and self-love degenerated into a perverse egoism.[92]

Attentive Christians would have seen as much and understood what was wrong with Rome, but Augustine knew that the faithful found it just as hard as pagans did to swim against prevailing currents. He likened coreligionists' compulsion to conform in late antiquity to earlier Christians' difficulty giving up the fellowship of synagogues in which they were nurtured. They were of the faith, although insufficiently moved by faith to become refugees and pilgrims.[93] But Augustine could register "the synagogue problem"

---

[91] Augustine, *civ.* 4.4.
[92] For Augustine's assessments, see the synopsis in Gaetano Lettieri, *Il senso della storia in Agostino d'Ippona: Il "saeculum" e la gloria nel "De Civitate Dei"* (Rome: Borla, 1988), 215–17.
[93] Augustine, *Io. ev. tr.* 93.2.

as solved. He could not, however, put to rest as easily the dilemma he faced as he tried to move the faithful to abjure their passion for praise and the will to win or simply to fit in—on this world's terms. They came to their churches but also to pagans' pageants, theaters, amphitheaters, and civic ceremonies, which captivated and acculturated spectators, making them good citizens.

Ordinary Christians were seldom welcomed into the best seats or into the upper tiers of Roman provincial society. Still, at the spectacles, they witnessed leading citizens descend, so to speak, drunk, disorderly and debauched in the arenas and in the streets at the conclusion of main events. Games, gladiators, races, performances, and pageants were the occasions for displays of idolatry, inebriation, and immorality. Proconsuls encouraged their legates to promote festivities, which Augustine saw as another, ominous symptom of what was wrong with Rome. Spectators and playgoers confused glitter and thrills with glory; actors and gladiators showed no shame as they courted audiences' affection. Patrons, as sponsors of actors, fighters, and racers, put on the shows to show off their wealth and status. Satchels of *sestertii* subsidized lewd and largely inconsequential exercises, all to boast about patrons' stations, players' prowess, and a city's standing.[94] Augustine made short work of parishioners' excuse that their absences would signal disrespect for the performers, athletes, and sponsors. They must worry less about offending the impresarios of idolatrous spectacles, he lectured, and worry more about offending God. If only Christians stayed away, Augustine predicted, the desolation of near-empty arenas (*tanta solitudo*) would reduce attendance and discourage patrons from paying for disgraceful recreations.[95] But could they stay away? What one could call late antiquity's entertainment industry, "producing glory," Agamben

---

[94] For proconsular encouragement, see Christophe Hugoniot, "Les légats du proconsul d'Afrique à la fin du IVe siècle et au début du Ve ap. J.-C. à la lumière des sermons et lettres d'Augustin," in *L'Africa romana: Lo spazio marittimo del Mediterraneo occidentale geografia storica ed economia*, ed. Mustapha Khanoussi, Paolo Ruggeri, and Cinzia Vismara (Rome: Carocci, 2002), 270–72. For Augustine's disgust, ep. 17.4 and ep. 29.5.
[95] Augustine, s. 301A.2.

might say, seemed to Augustine to have traumatized Christians. Their souls were sick.[96]

Their fascination with staged obscenities was one symptom. The fanaticism (*insania*) that drove fans to cheer or jeer gladiators and charioteers was another. Spectators were addicted, and Augustine was exasperated, wondering what was to be done.[97] His analysis of how crowds were working was rather sophisticated. Bonds between spectators were forged by shared loyalties to actors in character or to charioteers in circuses. The enthusiasms were infectious. But he believed such loyalties and loves should not be the results of contagion. One ought to know what, why, and whom one praises or heckles, he preached, adding that not knowing turned stadium crowds into moronic masses.[98] He recalled that his friend Alypius, reluctantly accompanying colleagues to the amphitheater, had been determined to remain detached. He closed his eyes, yet the sounds around him made Alypius curious. So he opened his eyes to the blood and brutality, and, despite his resolve, he could not turn away. Augustine editorialized: Alypius was, in a sense, possessed; no longer one individual who agreed to join a muster of others, he became a creature of the crowd.[99]

Soon after he became bishop, Augustine claimed that the games in Hippo were all but defunct (*talia paene defecerunt*).[100] His subsequent remarks about the popularity of spectacles suggest otherwise, but he was preaching at the time in Bulla Regia, midway between his diocese and Carthage, where—and apparently in Bulla Regia—the situation displeased him. The circus in Carthage could accommodate seventy thousand spectators; the Carthaginian amphitheater could seat half as many. Few provincial venues in the empire could boast such capacity. And the large crowds meant countless catalysts drawing colleagues into danger or, as Augustine

---

[96] Augustine, s. 9.10; Agamben, *Il Regno la Gloria*, 254–55.
[97] Augustine, *en. Ps.* 39.8; Augustine, *civ.* 8.5.
[98] Augustine, *en. Ps.* 53.10; Augustine, s. 90.6.
[99] Augustine, *conf.* 6.8.13: *Ut enim vidit illum sanguinem immanitatem simul ebibit et non se avertit, sed fixit aspectum et hauriebat furias et nesciebat et delectabatur scelere certaminis et cruenta voluptate inebriabatur. Et non erat iam ille, qui venerat, sed unus de turba, ad quem venerat, et verus eorum socius, a quibus adductus erat. Spectavit, clamavit, exarsit, abstulit inde secum insaniam.*
[100] Augustine, s. 310A.7.

said, sickness. He knew—or guessed—their best lines, and numbers made them seem reasonable: why not do as others do (*quare non facis quod faciunt*)?[101] Numbers also encouraged the patrons who paid and opulently clothed charioteers to exhibit their own exalted status and wealth. They paid favorites to fight one another and, increasingly in late antiquity, to fight wild animals. Combat delighted crowds and, Augustine imagined, the devil as well (*plaudente diabolo*). Moreover, spectacles diverted money that should have alleviated the plight of the poor; depravity trumped charity.[102] To those instructing catechumens, he sent a simple message to pass along with the intention of helping them help him wean students from idolatrous entertainments: Christians who coveted neither wealth nor status but were fond of spectacles mistook madness for pleasure.[103] Augustine referred to the glory that patrons, participants, and audiences were chasing as fools' glory (*gloria stultorum*). But he calculated that the world was full of fools. He packed into sermons bursts of invective and cutting caveats to convince congregants that theatrical and athletic extravagances dishonored those who paid for them, played in them, and flocked to them.[104]

One of Augustine's sermons suggests that funds were squandered when used to purchase grounds or build stadiums as well as to pay actors and gladiators. The expenditures on undignified entertainments proved only that financiers cared inordinately about making excellent impressions on their peers and about keeping citizens, distracted, awed, and docile. All who spent on (or at) circuses and amphitheaters, Augustine preached, were worldly, not godly.[105] But even among the worldly, an occasional official was known to have frowned on excess. Augustine's *City* has kind words for a consul, who, centuries earlier, persuaded the Roman Senate to discontinue its plan to expand the seating at one stadium. Had lust for power not been intense and pervasive at the time, Augustine mused, civic spectacles might have then been forbidden altogether,

---

[101] Augustine, *en. Ps.* 93.20. For statistics on seating, see Daniel G. Van Slyke, "The Devil and His Pomps in Fifth-Century Carthage: Renouncing *Spectacula* with Spectacular Imagery," *Dumbarton Oaks Papers* 59 (2005), 58.
[102] Augustine, s. 360B.20.
[103] Augustine, *cat. rud.* 16.25.
[104] See, for example, Augustine, s. 21.10 and Augustine, *en. Ps.* 149.10.
[105] Augustine, s. 32.20.

and what was wrong with Rome might not have been quite as conspicuous in buildings and in the boasting associated with them and the barbarities staged in them.[106]

History and humility

Augustine's *City of God* is, among other things, a tendentious history. Thanks to Sallust, Cicero, and Varro, among others, its repossession of the Roman republic's and empire's pasts is fairly well informed. But, for the history of the eastern empires, he relied on Hebrew Scriptures, adding and editing to have them serve his purposes. From Genesis, he learned that Nimrod, the founder of Babel was known as *venator*—hunter or gladiator, a slayer (*exstinctor*) of the earth's creatures. The *City* proposes, without biblical backing, that Nimrod also built the infamous tower of Babel. Conceivably, the Genesis references to hunting and slaying called to Augustine's mind the gladiators and games that the capacious, majestic edifices in his time had been constructed to house.[107] He did not explicitly connect the legendary tower with stadiums in Rome or Carthage, but he did suggest, as we learned, that such edifices were monuments to architects' and patrons' arrogance. He depicted them as exercises in civic and self-glorification. Nimrod along with Babylon's citizens demonstrated in stone that they glorified themselves, not God. The Romans did the same, while pretending to honor their gods.[108]

Babylon's tower toppled, but Augustine did not suggest its fate prefigured that of the amphitheaters and circuses of his time, perhaps because panic during the fourth and early fifth centuries was already widespread. To remind Romans of the current crisis after Emperor Valens's defeat at Adrianople in 378—and especially after Alaric's descent into Italy and sack of Rome in 410—might prompt paralysis just when churches and empire needed defending. Besides, Rome's history, as Augustine learned from his sources, was quite complicated. Its pageants had survived the best times—and

---

[106] Augustine, *civ.* 1.30-31.
[107] Augustine, *civ.* 16.4, citing Gen. 10:9.
[108] Augustine, *civ.* 16.10 and 17.4.

the worst.¹⁰⁹ With passions for praise and the lust for domination always at the center of Rome's history of expansion, civil unrest, and contraction, the empire's stadiums still stood as monuments to dominance, prosperity, ambition, decadence, and decline.¹¹⁰

Decadence and decline were predictable. No empire had been or could ever be exempt from the perpetual perishing that afflicted the terrestrial city. Naturally, Rome and Babylon were within the precincts of that "city." But not every citizen was destined to perish; Augustine trusted that, alongside what he characterized as a *consensio impietatis*—into which those who funded the building of stadiums fit as well as the fanatical citizens who crowded into them—there existed a *consensio pietatis*—pilgrims and misfits.¹¹¹ The ranks of the impious, he believed, were losing numbers as regeneration won over citizens of the terrestrial city to the celestial. He realized that God was the author of regeneration, yet he would not have denied that the faith of the faithful as well as the hope and love evident in their communities, along with the pastors' counsel and preachers' exhortations, encouraged some unbelievers to take hold of the lifeline God offered them.¹¹² To be sure, Augustine conceded, impiety would never become extinct this side of the grave. And he did not expect the pious to tear down towers and stadiums to build a kingdom of God on earth. To the contrary, and notwithstanding the confidence he had in the regeneration of many lost souls, he warned that the terrestrial city's predictable but, in this perverse, precarious world, utterly unreasonable preoccupations with greed and glory would seep into the tissues of the *consensio pietatis* and render pilgrims worldly and ungodly.¹¹³ On Augustine's instruction, therefore, catechumens were told that the Christians' captivity in Babylon would end and their susceptibilities to temptation (as well as temptations themselves) would expire only in the world to come.¹¹⁴ Until then, he preached, only fools bid for immortality

---

[109] Augustine, *civ.* 3.18.
[110] See Augustine, *civ.* 18.45, where Augustine's capsule analysis of sedition and dissolution at the end of the republic can stand as his appraisal of the third- and fourth-century empire as well.
[111] Augustine, s. Dolbeau 4.8.
[112] Augustine, *en Ps.* 86.6.
[113] Augustine, *en. Ps.* 125.3; Augustine, *civ.* 19.24.
[114] Augustine, *cat. rud.* 11.16.

subsidizing games to shore up their reputations. Patronage could not camouflage—it just documented—their immorality. In their present pelts, they loved the world too much.[115] To the extent that was true, they were captives in the cities of this world, the story of which was, as Augustine told it, and as historian Gregory Lee summarizes, a "[his]story of the world's two greatest empires, Assyria / Babylon and Rome. The empires, in turn, [were] political manifestations of lust, pride, and violence, all of which ar[o]se from an inordinate love for earthly goods."[116] And when loss beset such love, especially in the run up to and after 410, pagans and Christians alike would find the run-down appearance of the western empire troubling. The faithful had mistaken their faith's relatively good fortune during the reigns of several Christian emperors since the early fourth century as a promising sign that God would consistently award them temporal prerogatives, benefits, and security. For his part, Augustine preached against expectations of that sort soon after he started delivering sermons, urging parishioners not to be seduced by this life's turn-ons including love of country.[117]

Patriotism tended to displease him. He found Vergil at the source of Romans' patriotism and complained that the poet's inspiring prognosis—that their empire was *sine fine*, eternal—was misleading. Empires were among this world's perishables, Augustine pronounced, and the glory earned by citizens' love of honor and *patria* would not wholly console elites who had sacrificed to preserve or change political cultures. Indeed, love for the terrestrial cities only stirred persons with different versions of what such love should require—and from different cities—to murder each other.[118] Their loves and the civic pageants commemorating their lives were, Augustine claimed, love of self (*amor sui*) amplified. Threaded through the expressions of such love was what he described as "an old song" pretending one's *patria* was indestructible. But *patria* was

---

[115] Augustine, *Io. ev. tr.* 25.15.
[116] Gregory W. Lee, "Republics and their Loves: Rereading *City of God* 19," *Modern Theology* 27 (2011), 565.
[117] Augustine, s. 302.7: *blanditias male amatae . . . vitae*.
[118] Augustine, *civ.* 3.16 discusses Junius Brutus's murder of his two sons to preserve the fragile arrangements that attended the early republic, that is, the substitution of consuls for kings.

perishable, he protested; for true transcendence and glory, one must look to Christianity.[119]

The glory linked with temporal achievements and advantages was, no doubt, real and appealing, and elites had long stabled lame excuses for honoring it as eternal. Patrons of civic pageants and games trotted them out to beguile spectators. But the glory that was eternal was something vastly different from Rome's or Babylon's. It belonged to no province or metropolis—and to no public servant extolling relatively unremarkable achievements as if they testified to a deity's favor. By the grace of the Christians' God, glory belonged to their faith's martyrs whose sacrifices the churches' feasts commemorated.[120] The martyrs were glorious—yet self-effacing. They were glorious because they were self-effacing. In Christians' memories, the glory *of* the martyrs was, Augustine assured, the glory God promised *to* the martyrs and to the faithful devoted to preserving memories of the martyrs' humility and self-sacrifices.[121]

In sermons delivered long before he wrote about Christianity's martyrs in his *City* and in multiple sections of that text, Augustine redefined glory. In effect, the redefinition was a reversal. Persecutors who assumed they served to preserve the glory of their regimes as well as their gods' glory became victims and villains; the long gone were humbled by history, and those still alive were haunted by their consciences. But persecutors' victims became the victors. They were the apostles' successors and among the preeminent citizens of the city of God.[122] The martyrs were glorified by their suffering—another reversal—and by their refusals to capitulate to demands that they conform to the ways of this wicked world. Augustine pounced: the conclusion was obvious, he said; persecution had not been the ruin of the church but the making of it.[123]

The reversal of expectations about glory started with Jesus's selection of his disciples; he chose from among the poor and powerless, not from the ranks of the rich and powerful. And his

---

[119] Augustine, *en. Ps.* 149.1-2.
[120] Augustine, s. 335E.2: *Gloria martyrum in eorum sollemnitatibus ab hominibus adverti potest.*
[121] Augustine, *en. Ps.* 144.7.
[122] Augustine, *en. Ps.* 56.16; Augustine, *civ.* 5.14 and 8.26-27.
[123] Augustine, *civ.* 10.21.

choice, Augustine explained, was to show that the marginal, not the magnificent, were well placed and best qualified to convey effectively the good news of redemption. Blustery self-assertion, love of praise, and lust for domination—none of which afflicted the fishermen and ragged craftsmen whom Jesus called to follow him— kept prominent citizens from taking up crosses.[124] A pastoral letter to Hebrews attributed to the apostle Paul what Benjamin Dunning calls "outsider status." *Hebrews* commends a "self-conscious positioning of the Christian self as other," an "alterity" that couples glory with the world's "reproach." *Hebrews*, Dunning says, had urged readers to forsake "the pleasures" of citizenship to become pilgrims or "sojourners."[125]

To forsake those pleasures was, for Augustine, to confound the world, as the Christian martyrs had for more than three centuries. He directed the faithful to honor their faith's martyrs, not just by commemorating their courage but by imitating it.[126] Yet this call for imitation called for clarification, because the martyrs discounted not only what the world considered glorious but also what it assessed as good. Taking health as his example, Augustine explained that Christians need not let themselves go to seed to honor their martyrs but should be gratified that God's love for them gave the martyrs courage, *in extremis*, to disregard the good—health and safety—to pursue something better.[127]

As turmoil across the Mediterranean drove refugees to Africa, Augustine addressed the frightening, if less extreme, predicaments facing the faithful who fled. Their misfortunes were hardly unforeseeable. The western empire had been in trouble for generations. Yet refugees brooded about possessions, loved and lost, and apparently questioned their God's caretaking. Augustine told them to use the crisis as a chance to reprioritize, to confess their sin in having become so attached to perishable things of this world.[128] In a

---

[124]Augustine, s. 87.12.
[125]Dunning, *Aliens and Sojourners*, 54–55, commenting on Heb. 11-13.
[126]Augustine, s. 325.1; Augustine, *Io. ev. tr.* 7.17 (*confundere mundum*).
[127]Augustine, s. 306D.4: *contemnat bonum ut veniat ad melius*.
[128]Augustine, *civ.* 1.10: *illi autem infirmiores, qui terrenis his bonis . . . aliquantula tamen cupiditate cohaerebant, quantum haec amando peccaverint, perdendo senserunt. . . . Oportet enim ut eis adderetur etiam experimentorum disciplina, a quibus tam diu fuerat neglecta.*

sermon likely preached before Rome's humiliation in 410 yet while Italy and other parts of the western empire were being overrun, he conceded that the martyrs' detachment would seem lunacy to most whose interest in power, praise, and possessions was undisturbed. But those refugees, who questioned the martyrs' sanity, on careful reflection—for which his sermon was to lay the groundwork—ought to realize that the martyrs' madness was soteriologically sane and glorious. The *gloria martyrum* was far more lasting than the glory gained by soldiers sacrificing for the safety or prestige of terrestrial cities. The martyrs' glory was incomparable. Agamben sees that it radiated to and through the messianic communities whenever the memories of martyrs' sacrifices were honored alongside those of Jesus and the apostles; Augustine believed the martyrs' glory would last as long as terrestrial cities survived and thereafter, everlastingly, in the celestial city.[129]

The last claim posed a problem, and Augustine took what might be described as evasive action to arrive at a satisfactory solution. He denied that the martyrs sought celebrity afforded by the commemorations of their sacrifices. They preferred that the faithful confer glory on God who gave them courage and contentment. Augustine had the martyrs reminding admirers of the power of God's love, and he helped, adding that commemorations ought to associate the martyrs' glory with their humility. They ought also, he counseled, to impart the lesson that the devotion to self-promotion, by contrast, was appallingly irreverent and offensive. It never let the arrogant rest. Restlessness was their lot along with a ravenous hunger for praise and a lust for power, all of which was what was wrong with Rome.[130]

Des bienfaits de Dieu[131]

Augustine often repeated that Jesus, the first Christian martyr, was Christianity's best lesson in humility and the pathway to knowledge

---

[129]Augustine, s. 335C.11; Agamben, *Il Regno e la Gloria*, 254–55.
[130]See Augustine, *civ.* 5.14, drawing from Jn 12.43 and Mt. 6.1, and Augustine, *en. Ps.* 118(12).3.
[131]See Hombert, *Gloria Gratiae*, 352: *Sans doute l'anamnèse des bienfaits de Dieu est-elle inséparable de la mémoire de péché.*

about humanity's finitude and fallibility. Jesus's was the proper perspective on worldly and godly glory from which the faithful should learn how to be content and compassionate. The further encouragement they received from Augustine set the stage for revelations about their remorse, repentance, and regeneration.[132]

Sinners would have had no excuses. Sermons addressed anything in the gospels that the faithful found unintelligible. Sacraments sealed their gospels' promises. Persons misbehaving— much as if the "sun of righteousness" had not risen—were abominably in arrears. Their sins had mounted, despite God's pardon on offer.[133] So, as Gaetano Lettieri notices, Augustine called for more instruction and distinguished between the enlightenment from the "sun" (or Son) available to Christians and the wisdom pagans' philosophers promised. Augustine admitted that religious knowledge would not come to the faithful as swiftly, clearly, and incontrovertibly as pagan and Christian devotees of philosophy expected. The sun and Son may have risen, but the faithful would see their sins with difficulty at first. A fog would settle on them, but, Augustine assured, they would not get lost in the mists if only they abandoned the misperceptions that braced their boasting. Commenting on rough weather predicted in one of the Hebrew Bible's last psalms, his exposition scurries past the clouds, rain, frost, and snow, to turn the text into a hymn to humility, to self-abasement—a self-scourging self-analysis—and to repentance, which he numbered among God's benefactions.[134]

For the fog lifted when Christians' humility seemed sufficient. To whom? Augustine declined to specify, although he instructed the faithful to be fruitful, not simply in sorrow but also in compassion for others, which paid God's love for creation forward and which bishops could readily discern and measure.[135] God, he said, despised

---

[132] See, for example, Augustine, *civ.* 11.2; Augustine, s. 293.7; and Gerard Remy, "La notion de *Medietas* chez Saint Augustin," *RSR* 85 (2011), 219–20.

[133] See Augustine, *en. Ps.* 103(3).23 and *en. Ps.* 120.4, relying on Mal. 4.2 for the Son and "sun."

[134] Augustine, *en. Ps.* 147.24: *Ad hoc est ergo illa nebula, ut noveris nescire te, et noveris quid scire oporteat, et videas te invalidum ad illud sciendum quod oportet sciri. . . . Non erras in nebula; fide sequere. Sed quia conaris videre, et non potes, poeniteat te peccatorum.* Also see Lettieri, *Il senso della storia*, 156–57.

[135] Augustine, s. 72.3.

arrogance but raised up the humble and fruitful.¹³⁶ Probably, Augustine plumped for humility because that virtue corresponded to a truth he increasingly emphasized: none was sinless. The fog would lift, but humble penitents still struggled with inordinate desires, *sit veritas in pugna*.¹³⁷ Their base nature tempted them to stray and, we now know, from Augustine's perspective, to boast, should their waywardness lead them to what the world measured as successes. So he asked: burdened by the flesh, were they any better than grubs?¹³⁸ Perhaps he asked that question during unrecorded exchanges with parishioners. From what he reports about his diocesan court, one may infer he had ample opportunities. Refereeing disputes, he found litigants uncivil, unwilling to absolve neighbors for petty missteps, burdened with a sense of self-righteousness, and burdensome. Deaf to his sermons' pleas for compassion, rancorous suitors heaved accusations at each other, and the litigants who lost questioned his impartiality.¹³⁹ So, in 426, Augustine appears to have been pleased to hand over his bishop's court with other pastoral obligations related to mediation and arbitration (*refundere onera*) to his deacon and successor-designate. He told his congregation that he needed time for biblical study and exposition—and for polemic.¹⁴⁰

He was free in semi-retirement to contemplate God's many benefactions. But, almost immediately, he plunged into battles that began when the Pelagians' opinions were aired in a monastery at Hadrumentum. He wrote to the abbot to apply the apostle Paul's first letter to the Corinthians against the claim that grace was merited and, therefore, that meritorious Christians might boast of having received it.¹⁴¹ Augustine argued that merit could not matter in ways the Pelagians imagined. God's acceptance and affection were not rewards for moral endeavor. To insist they were amounted to excessive self-congratulation, which, he went on, was absolutely unwarranted. Whatever virtues Pelagius and his acolytes possessed—and Augustine occasionally was willing to concede

---

¹³⁶Augustine, *en. Ps.* 93.16.
¹³⁷Augustine, s. 163.9.
¹³⁸Augustine, *Io. ev. tr.* 1.13, citing Ps 22.6: *Nam omnes homines de carne nascentes, quid sunt nisi vermes?*
¹³⁹Augustine, *en. Ps.* 25(2).13.
¹⁴⁰Augustine, ep. 213.5.
¹⁴¹Augustine, ep. 214.3-4.

the seriousness of their moral purposes—their righteousness had become too righteous (*multum justus*), presumptuous, and therefore unrighteous.[142]

They underestimated the pervasiveness sin. And their miscalculation kept them from what Augustine, throughout his career, touted as an invigorating, wholesome humility. Even before the Pelagians crossed to Africa, he referred his pagan correspondents to Jesus's exemplary self-deprecation as an antidote for pride, which he long held responsible for Romans' inglorious pursuit of glory and leading citizens' lust for domination.[143] Fast forward to similar arguments in Augustine's *City*, and one reasonably may assume Augustine bracketed the Pelagians (as well as Manichees we encountered in the last chapter) with pagan philosophers he addressed when he again prescribed humility as the cure for those whose self-proclaimed intelligence kept them from admitting their wretchedness—and from accepting God's grace.[144]

But posturing was prevalent. Philosophers, provincial officials, local patricians, and commoners during commercial transactions posed, and their posing, Augustine supposed, was among the chief obstacles to their flinching at their own arrogance. One of his sermons started by goading auditors to leap over or transcend the posturing that put modesty beyond their reach. But it finished by telling them to leap over themselves.[145] Other obstacles, of course, attached to their self-importance, which required constant maintenance, specifically, for Augustine, the inordinate desires to acquire, preserve, and increase worldly goods and worldly glory—desires that tethered citizens to secular standards for success.

---

[142]See Augustine, *Io. ev. tr.* 95.2 (*ipso nimio fit injustus*) and Augustine, *c. Iul. Imp.* 5.61.

[143]Augustine, ep. 232.6: *Quoniam ergo a vanitate superbiae prius ad humilitatem deponendi sumus, ut inde surgentes solidam celsitudinem teneamus. . . . Sic tandem animadvertit terrena superbia, nihil in ipsis terrenis esse potentius humilitate divina, ut etiam saluberrima humilitas humana contra insultantem sibi superbiam, divinae imitationis patrocinio tueretur.*

[144]Augustine, *civ.* 10.28: *Hoc* [Jesus crucified] *quasi stultum et infirmum tamquam sua virtute sapientes fortesque contemnunt. Sed haec est gratia, quae sanat infirmos, non superbe jactantes falsam beatitudinem suam, sed humiliter potius veram miseriam confitentes.*

[145]Augustine, *en. Ps.* 76.1 (*translire debemus quidquid nos impedit*) and 76.13 (*nos transiliamus*).

But persons became obstacles to themselves when they entertained the idea that they might overcome any obstacle—even "get over" themselves—without God's help. They banked on their virtuosity. There were exceptions, Augustine admitted, yet, he mourned, too few knew or had a clue what self-transcendence meant. Their prayers for a healthy crop, a profitable exchange, a full coffer, or a formidable reputation assumed that benefactions (*bienfaits de Dieu*) could be measured as material security or lofty status. They would continue moving sideways rather than forward until they realized that their unanswered prayers were the best of God's blessings. For—prosperity deferred or denied—the prayerful, Augustine supposed, once they were assisted by their pastors and preachers, might see how inappropriate their prayers had been and learn how to pray and what to hope for.[146] They would come to live as pilgrims and to discount what the pagans and Pelagians around them thought glorious. And they would pray to come (or for the stamina to remain) among the faithful on pilgrimage in time, heading for a city about which glorious things were said in sacred texts (*gloriosa dictu*).[147]

Domenico Marafioti is likely right: readers without profound religious commitment may nowadays be more puzzled than persuaded by what came to be Augustine's abiding conviction that worldly glory was antithetical to godly glory, but Augustine, Marafioti concedes, believed the dichotomy unproblematic. He expected catechumens only loosely familiar with Christian culture would find it intelligible and, in time, moving.[148] At least, they ought to discover in the lessons he prepared for them and for those instructing them how they could and why they should leap over themselves and over the protocols of one "society" to take up the values of another, the church.[149] Writing directly to a catechumen

---

[146] Augustine, ep. 140.19.
[147] Augustine, *civ.* 11.1.
[148] Marafioti, "Come leggere," 249–51.
[149] Augustine, *cat. rud.* 19.31: *Omnes enim homines amantes superbiam et temporalem dominationem cum vano typho et pompa arrogantiae, omnesque spiritus qui talia diligunt, et gloriam suam subjectione hominum quaerunt, simul una societate devincti sunt; et si saepe adversum se pro his rebus dimicant, pari tamen pondere cupiditatis in eamdem profunditatem praecipitantur, et sibi morum et meritorum similitudine conjunguntur. Et rursus omnes homines et omnes spiritus*

rather than to colleagues guiding him, he dreamed up a crisis. His protagonist was fairly pious—not purposefully delinquent—yet, if we may extrapolate from the questions he posed to Augustine, fond of quality brands and a few guilty pleasures and fearful that his taste for both of the latter would lead to loss. What might stay the blow and prop up piety? Ordinarily, Augustine interpreted such anxiety as punishment. In this instance, he took a different tack. He consoled his correspondent, recasting the anxieties of his character and his correspondent as therapy, which eventually would diminish their desire for temporal goods. They would understand what to pray for and what were the most valuable benefactions of God as they found lasting comfort in the contrast between earthly felicity and celestial beatitude and as they recalled how Job, Jesus, and Christianity's martyrs overcame anguish.[150]

The contrast had significant bearing as or after persons negotiated the leaps Augustine prescribed. Yet the image of leaping is misleading. It calls to mind something acrobatic and the skill of a well-coached gymnast. To prevent Pelagians inferring as much, Augustine, as we now know, stressed that Christians could neither count on their strength and agility nor depend upon the compelling character of preachers' (as coaches') sermons to establish the faith and love that enabled self-transcendence. Only God, within, deposited both, enabling the faithful, humble, and compassionate to leap over the beguiling prospect of worldly advantage and worldly glory. Only God, within, could inspire repentance and awaken a desire for God's glory.[151] Augustine, prior to the Pelagian controversy—and despite his deference to divine providence in the *Confessions*—was emphatic: in an early treatise *De vera religione*, he put the divinely inspired rebirth of souls into a seven-tiered program that created the righteous, celestial, "interior" Christian (*homo interior et caelestius*); at different tiers or stages, persons abjured vulgar pleasures, less tenaciously pursued temporal advantages, devalued

---

humiliter Dei gloriam quaerentes, non suam, et eum pietate sectantes, ad unam pertinent societatem.

[150] Augustine, ep. 140.19-20, 33-35. Also, in this connection, consult Hombert, *Gloria Gratiae*, 110–11, discussing Augustine's s. 160.

[151] Augustine, *praed, sanct.* 7.12: *in vanum laborat praedicando aedificans fidem nisi eam Dominus miserando intus aedificat.*

protocols that preserved order in their terrestrial cities, celebrated their rebirth, and—at the culmination—consistently behaved compassionately. Leaps here, to say the least, were more like slight steps up and out from an inward regeneration toward behavioral implications that validated regeneration.[152]

Jews in the Hebrews' scriptures could be excused for having overlooked the need for inward regeneration and for having assumed their ability to fulfill the demands of God's law; Jesus had yet to appear. There was no possibility of following him.[153] Pagans would seem to have had a choice to forsake their gods, accept the remission of their sins and the one true God's gift within enabling them to leap, spring, or stride to freedom (*in veram emicans libertatem*), yet Augustine saw that they, just as the Pelagians and sinners of all stripes, needed—so he labored to supply—encouragement to salvage their souls.[154] But remember, for Augustine, strictly speaking, sinners were powerless to do so. Nor would they propel themselves over obstacles to repentance and redemption. Remember also that—Augustine, again—encouragement (or coaching) would be ineffective without God's movement into—and of—sinners' souls. He was never clearer on this count than when he concluded a section of his unfinished response to Julian of Eclanum. After flatly refusing to agree with his most persistent Pelagian opponent—that passages from his own treatises substantiated Julian's thinking about merit, righteousness earned rather than conferred as a kindness (*bienfait de Dieu*)—Augustine first appealed to Julian to implore God to grant him the desire for righteousness. Immediately after, he appealed to God to grant Julian the desire to implore God.[155]

That sequence neatly sums up the arguments Augustine threaded through this anti-Pelagian invective, some of which have already been reported in this chapter and might be summarized by repeating its (and his) indictment of the way the late Roman world conceived of glory, underestimating the seriousness of sin and the extent of

---

[152] Augustine, *vera rel.* 26.48-49.

[153] Augustine, *en. Ps.* 9.4.

[154] Augustine, *civ.* 2.29.

[155] Augustine, *c. Iul. imp.* 6.18: *Hanc Dei justitiam concupisce, O fili Juliane, noli in tua virtute confidere; hanc, inquam, Dei concupisce justitiam; quam donet tibi Dominus et habere.*

human disability. Rome construed its expanse and glory as gifts from their gods. But they were not, Augustine gravely replied; they were concessions from the Christians' God. Julian attributed moral fervor largely to human effort and looked for reward rather than longing for God's mercy. But only God—as benefactor—could grant that longing along with the desire for self-transcendence and the redemptive reorientation responsible for moral fervor.[156]

Augustine thought exaggerated self-esteem was not just theologically inappropriate but psychologically and socially destabilizing as well. Inflated egos were more likely to be bruised by slight humiliations and to misinterpret meaningless gestures as offenses.[157] When, unchallenged and unbruised, the sense of superior righteousness led to contempt for supposedly inferior others. Augustine presumed he had proof: the descendants of Christians who seceded from what became Catholic Christianity in the early fourth century and who, to his mind, uncharitably perpetuated a schism that unsettled Christianity in Africa. In principle, they categorically opposed inconstancy; in practice, if Augustine's chronicle of controversies dividing them can be trusted, they pardoned selectively to keep factions from tearing their sect into fractions. They vilified Catholic Christian clerics, allegedly enlisting thugs to intimidate critics. Augustine surely exaggerated secessionists' (Donatist Christians') pride and prejudices as well as the number of dissidents who approved of intimidation, yet their bishops do appear to have stubbornly rejected the overtures that he and his colleagues made to end the schism. Donatists' refusals to reconcile proved to him that they cared more about preserving the memory of an attempted coup generations earlier and about nursing their sense of injury that followed its failure than about the peace of the African provinces; the secessionists' pride made them vengeful and irrational. Cities and country estates were divided. Two Christian congregations quarreled where there should have been one.[158] Love and the lack of it had consequences. Donatists

---

[156] In this connection, see Alici, "*Interrogatio mea, intentio mea*: Le movement de la pensée augustinienne," 379–81.
[157] See Augustine, s. 142.12 and Augustine, *Io. ev. tr.* 29.8.
[158] See Augustine, *bapt.* 5.2; Augustine, *Cresc.* 3.60.66; Shaw, *Sacred Violence*, 732–35; and Kaufman, "Donatism Revisited: Moderates and Militants in Late Antique North Africa," *Journal of Late Antiquity* 2 (2009), 140–42.

faced official sanctions after Marcellinus, while still in good odor, adjourned the Council of Carthage, as we know, but Augustine, before and after, tried to save them from the worst. He opposed capital punishment and intimated that he would never endorse or enforce harsh corporal punishment.[159] He risked officials' displeasure with requests that Donatists' lives be spared. Still, he mounted no campaign for juridical reform. As Matthias Mayer points out, he was no reformer, although he spiritedly (*mutig*) declared how out of order the well-ordered systems of the terrestrial city were.[160]

The powerful were still wed to traditional concepts of glory and domination. Appeals to the contrast between terrestrial truths and religious or celestial truths—between worldly and godly glory—might get through to a few on the higher rungs of provincial government; Augustine knew better than to expect more. Nonetheless, he was intent on tamping down pride (*contundendam et edomandam superbiam*).[161] To do so, as we learned in this chapter, he arraigned the Roman polis and officials' sense of civic virtues. The premise, from which his protests developed was simple: "the certainties of virtuous action . . . could not [be] composed as reflections upon this world." Miles Hollingworth puts it quite well, and John Milbank justifiably adds that secular virtues, as Augustine never forgot, reflected the "sinful assertion of pride and domination [that] introduced a pervasive presence of conflict" into political cultures. The worldly could not rehabilitate—or even resurface—their world. Augustine winced at their efforts to hang halos over its offensive protocols.[162]

---

[159] Augustine, ep. 10*.4. For Augustine's many comments on proper punitive measures—including the punishment of Donatists—see my two recent studies, "Augustine's Punishments," *HTR* 109 (2016), 550–56 and "Punishment and Reconciliation: Augustine," in *Peace and Reconciliation in the Classical World*, ed. E. P. Molony and Michael Stuart Williams (London: Routledge, 2017), 271–84.

[160] Matthias Mayer, "Augustins' *De civitate Dei*: Philosophie der Geschichte oder Geschichte der Philosophie?" *Freiburger Zeitschrift für Philosophie und Theologie* 61 (2014), 427–28.

[161] Augustine, *div. qu.* 71.5; Augustine, s. 144.1.

[162] Consult John Milbank, *Theology and Social Theory: Beyond Secular Reason* (Oxford: Blackwell, 1990), 390–91 and Miles Hollingworth, *The Pilgrim City: St Augustine of Hippo and his Innovation in Political Thought* (London: T&T Clark, 2010), 208. Also see James Wetzel, "Splendid Vices and Secular Virtues: Variations on Milbank's Augustine," *JRE* 32 (2010), 280–81.

The profusion of contrasts between worldly and godly virtues and glory, which fill this chapter, seem to certify Hollingworth's and Milbank's judgments. But the caveat introduced by Christoph Horn is also critical: we must not think Augustine gravitated toward either cynicism or escapism.[163] His *City of God* should put doubts about that to rest. He sent copies to political officials, despite the text's criticisms of political culture. Marcellinus received a copy of its first few books before falling victim during an intrigue, which we now know was not unlike those we saw the *City*'s historical sections chronicle. Augustine sent the *City* to Firmus, proconsular legate in Carthage.[164] He apparently thought a few political officials worth enlightening and saving, even if political cultures were beyond reclamation. And he deposited in his *City* the glaring exception to his rule that the powerful were contemptuous of the humble and stubbornly self-important: the public penance of Emperor Theodosius. Augustine was keen to plug the episode and emperor as well into one of his many sermons commending humility to parishioners and posterity.[165]

Might the Theodosius exception have suggested a new rule to Augustine? His *City* records a select number of the emperor's achievements. The regime's anti-pagan edicts feature prominently, as does his supposedly scrupulous protection of Catholic Christian prelates against their anti-Nicene and Donatist critics. But, to Augustine, nothing was more sensational than the emperor's display of humility, for Theodosius set aside his regalia while asking to be pardoned, which suggested to Augustine that appeasing God meant more to him than ruling the world.[166]

The emperor's entourage may have interpreted the episode differently. Conceivably, they feared their retainer's humility would be construed as humiliation. Or might they have suspected that, as André Tuliere contends, the drama had been staged by Bishop Ambrose and Theodosius to keep the public in awe. Certainly,

---

[163]Christoph Horn, "Augustinus über politische Ethik und legitime Staatsgewalt," in *Augustinus: Recht und Gewalt*, ed. Cornelius Mayer (Würzburg: Echter, 2010), 51.
[164]Augustine, ep. 2*.2; Hugoniot, "Les légats," 2080–81.
[165]Augustine, *civ.* 5.26; Augustine, s. 392.3.
[166]Compare the account of Theodosius's penance in Ambrose, *De obitu Theodosii*, 34 with the account in Augustine, *civ.* 5.26.

Christians might otherwise have questioned the sincerity of their emperor's faith because, as Jörg Ernesti documents, he was known to have appointed pagan proconsuls, relied on the leadership and loyalty of pagans and anti-Nicene Christians in his army, and commenced courting senators whose striking tributes to him were reminiscent of Rome's former imperial cults.[167] Predictably, Augustine overlooked whatever evidence existed of the emperor's affection for some pagans and their affection for him. Perhaps Theodosius stumped him, as he has stumped scholars. Yet we know Augustine retained the Theodosius exception as an exception, deploying it to show the most powerful figure in government practicing humility—to feature the part crisis played bringing the emperor to his knees. For crises were critical to the *City's* claim— and to Augustine's arguments in sermons and correspondence— that God's power over the powerful demonstrated that lovers of this world mistook their empire's expanse, its provinces' prosperity, and their peers' envy for genuine glory.[168]

Without crisis, there could be no convalescence. When pagans in the city of Calama, a long day's ride from Hippo, asked Augustine to intervene and have their city's bishop abort his suit for punitive damages, he declined. The pagans attacked the local church and clergy but had expressed regret afterward. Still, Augustine advised that the merciful course was to let the crisis play out. Pagans should pay compensatory *and* punitive damages. Hardships occasioned by the latter followed by repentance would ensure that remorse was not feigned to spare the offenders' purses.[169] When Goths sacked Rome a few years later, he similarly construed the crisis as therapeutic. Shock, he trusted, would move Christians and pagans alike to recognize how impermanent and untrustworthy this world's honors—and pleasures—were (*omnes saeculi vanitates*). And that would incline them to reevaluate the respective values of worldly

---

[167] Jörg Ernesti, *Princeps Christianus und Kaiser aller Römer: Theodosius der Grosse im Lichte zeitgenössischer Quellen* (Paderborn: Schöningh, 1998), 82–87, 349–50; André Tuliere, "La politique de Théodose le Grand et les évêques de la fin du IVᵉ siècle," *Vescovi e pastori in epoca teodosiana*, vol. 1 (Rome: Institutum Patristicum Augustinianum, 1997), 61–71.
[168] Augustine, *civ.* 5.14-17; Augustine, *en. Ps.* 65.4.
[169] Augustine, ep. 104.9-10.

glory and godly glory.[170] Crisis had become indispensable; without crisis, there could be no convalescence—and no repentance. John Milbank seems quite correct, suggesting Augustine came to see "no point [in] laying down Christian norms for an area which was intrinsically sinful."[171]

So the best course was to create an atypical ruler, the *City*'s Theodosius, to shock typical magistrates into raising questions about their conduct that admit of no easy and soothing answer. Agamben's introduction of the Spiritual Franciscans' nonconformity serves a similar purpose, raising issues with the forms of life prescribed by— and "lived under [—] regime[s] of maximal consumption."[172] But unlike Agamben, Augustine occasionally wrote as though typical civic virtues could serve as a foundation on which Christian virtues might construct and consecrate more humane terrestrial cities. He suggested as much in a letter to Marcellinus, though he also denounced public life as a cesspit (*colluvi[um] morum pessimorum*) in the same document and depicted Christianity as something of an escape from the flow of sewage.[173] Yet his *City* leaves little doubt that Christianity mandates a strategic withdrawal (*sensim subtrahit*), a decathect (or temperamental disengagement) from the world that, despite the civic spirit ostensibly displayed in public spectacles, was being consumed by corruption (*tabescenti ac labenti*).[174]

Robert Dodaro, therefore, may be overreaching when he proposes to reconstitute "an Augustinian model of the just society" from Augustine's remarks on political and theological virtues. Christoph Horn may have a better grip on the bishop's so-called "political theology" when he presumes Augustine was resigned to enduring political cultures that were functionally necessary yet morally inadequate.[175] Daniel Burns's comments on one of Augustine's dialogues on free choice seem to illustrate both the necessity and the inadequacy. In the treatise, probably composed

---

[170]Augusitne, *exc. urb.* 9.
[171]Milbank, *Theology and Social Theory*, 407.
[172]See W. Scott Blanchard, "Forms of Power, Forms of Life: Agamben's Franciscan Turn," *New Literary History* 46 (2015), 530.
[173]Augustine, ep. 138.10, 14, and 17.
[174]Augustine, *civ.* 2.18.
[175]Compare Horn, "Augustinus über politische Ethik," 60–62 with Dodaro, *Christ and the Just Society*, 106–7.

in two stages, and certainly before Augustine became bishop, interlocutor Evodius confides that earthly legislation, which reflects God's will, has a high moral purpose and should secure more than a modicum of justice. Laws are God's and society's fists. Punishments promote restraint; God, reinforcing civility, aligned civic piety with religious piety. Augustine's responses do not deny Evodius's point about the importance of lawmaking and law enforcement, that is, the probability that laws deter crime. But his answers to Evodius maintain that God's eternal law transcends politics and, as Burns says, cannot be "instantiated in any temporal legal code."[176]

Eternal law—along with God's love and the gift of faith—were "instantiated" in the faithful, alerting them to God's beneficence—*des bienfaits de Dieu*—while reconciling them, Augustine said, to their roles as pilgrims (*in via nondum in patria*).[177] Sojourners in time and captives in Babylon, they were not to adopt their leaders' passions for conquest and, he would have it, were to anticipate their release in other than juridical terms. For Augustine, then, knowledge of their captivity was one of those *bienfaits de Dieu* that draw pilgrims from the corrupting effects of convention.[178]

It bears repeating that he was under no illusion that the withdrawal or disengagement he countenanced was easily achieved. Churches in late antiquity were not free of the pressures that made the world around them tricky and risky to navigate. Manichees, Donatists, Pelagians, and pagans boasted to break the silence and, presumably, to show onlookers how invested they were in virtue and in the resuscitation of their cults or sects or civic pageants. Augustine admitted that the Catholic Christian exegetes who opposed them occasionally were too self-assertive.[179] For his part, he never wearied of emphasizing the importance of humility and of pitting godly glory against the inglorious lusts for glory and

---

[176]Daniel Burns, "Augustine on the Moral Significance of Human Law," *Revue d'études augustiniennes et patristiques* 61 (2015), 292–97, studying *De libero arbitrio*, especially 1.13-16 and 1.31-34.

[177]Augustine, s. 103.1.

[178]Augustine, *civ.* 19.17: *dum apud terrenam civitatem velut captivam vitam suae peregrinationis agit. . . . peregrinam colligit societatem, non curans quidquid in moribus, legibus, institutisque diversum est.* For sojourners' decathect, also see Augustine, *Io. ev. tr.* 124.5.

[179]Augustine, *Cresc.* 1.7.9; Augustine, *en. Ps.* 118(1).2.

domination in this wicked world. From the start of his ministry, he featured the incarnation as a model. Jesus's virtues as well as his Cross were useful, as was the *gloria martyrum*, to encourage patience, fortitude, sacrifice, and humility, but the magnitude of God's sacrifice—his becoming fully human in the incarnation—was Augustine's beacon lighting the way for the faithful, showing them what was required of them as humble pilgrims.[180]

Humility, however, does not prohibit pilgrims from conjuring alternative poleis. One can peg humility as a critical first step in deactivation. It prompts a disenchantment with, profanation of, and disengagement from sovereign powers' spectacles and protocols, channeling citizens into an assortment of inauthentic forms of life. Augustine and Agamben would agree on that much, and introducing Hannah Arendt into their conversation may enable us to appreciate better its radical political implications for pilgrims, refugees, and pariahs, who, all three theorists suggested, were well positioned to perceive the limits of renovation and possibilities for innovation.

---

[180] Augustine, *div. qu.* 80.2-3; Hombert, *Gloria Gratiae*, 442–44.

3

Arendt's Augustine

To Augustine and not to Augustine

Hannah Arendt wrote her doctoral dissertation on Augustine's concept of love under the direction of Karl Jaspers, whom she later declared to have been the only person to have educated her.[1] She exaggerated, and this final chapter explains why Augustine ought to be reserved a special place among the others from whom she drew ideas and inspiration. Arendt was critical of him, but it is difficult to deny that, as she pondered twentieth-century pariahs and poleis, he haunted her frustrations with the practice of politics and, arguably, her reflections on alternatives to the public realm, frustrations and reflections that have a tremendous bearing on how one might read Augustine as a radical. As disenchantment set in, as Arendt found that "action and speech," "the highest activities in the political realm," were undermined by bureaucracies, she questioned whether the public realm was the best place to reclaim "the potentiality which springs up between people when they come together in action and speech."[2]

Arendt concluded her dissertation contemplating ever so briefly the social consequences of what she identified as Augustine's estrangement (*Entfremdung*) from the political competition that

---

[1] *Hannah Arendt-Karl Jaspers: Briefwechsel, 1926-1969*, ed. Lotte Köhler and Hans Saner (Munich: Piper, 1985), 368: *Sie der einige Mensch, der mich erzogen hat.*
[2] Arendt, *The Human Condition*, 2nd ed. (Chicago: The University of Chicago Press, 1988), 22–24, 206–9.

glory hounds around him seemed to relish. He sometimes sounded forlorn, but Arendt noted that his recoil led him to advocate new sorts of cohorts alongside and, in some ways, opposed to prevailing political conduct and commercial protocols in late antiquity (*ein neues Miteinander und Füreinander . . . neben und gegen*).³ As we learned, he tried intermittently—and with a few partial successes— to organize unconventional, alternative poleis. But circumstances in Italy and, from the 390s, clerical commitments in Africa led him to scuttle several experiments. Setbacks in Rome, Milan, and Thagaste, though, did not deter him from retrying in Hippo—and from forming the conventual community that later impressed Agamben. Arendt chose not to write about those efforts, and at least one reviewer complained about that choice and about her neglect of her subject's sources.⁴ But Arendt was not writing historical theology, and she cared little for the social history of late antiquity. Still, what she learned—and conveyed clearly at the end of her dissertation— was that Augustine harbored no hope for the renovation of Roman provincial or imperial government. He innovated, but Arendt held his innovations to have been unworldly and irresponsible until she began losing her faith in the possibility that the public realm would allow for forgiveness, tolerance, virtue, promise keeping, and new beginnings.

Her faith in the public realm had been tested soon after—and long after—she completed her dissertation in 1929. She watched as elites in Germany during the 1930s all but abandoned government in Germany to a tyrant and flattered his collaborators as they shaped their hideously hegemonic regime. Fascists there drove her into exile, eventually to the United States, where she wrote perceptively about intolerance in Europe. Arendt imagined that, in large part, intellectuals' indifference to developments in beer halls and backrooms ceded the hearts and minds of German, Austrian,

---

³Arendt, *Der Liebesbegriff bei Augustin*, 86. Commentary by Joanna Vecchiarelli Scott and Judith Chelius Stark, "Rediscovering Hannah Arendt," in their edition and translation of revisions she proposed late in her career, put this idea in context; see Arendt, *Love and Saint Augustine* (Chicago: University of Chicago Press, 1996), especially 152–54.
⁴See Max Zepf's review of Arendt's *Liebesbegriff*, in *Gnomon* 8 (1932), 104–5.

Italian, and Russian citizens to bullying despots. She suspected that sensible political participation would have averted the tragedies associated with authoritarian regimes in Europe during the 1940s and would be required to prevent the world from going mad yet again; so no wonder, Augustine's alternative communities seemed irresponsible. He relied on compassion (*Miteinander und Füreinander*) to keep them viable, but Arendt confided to her journal that people of action mistrusted love. As we shall see, she explained why more systematically in essays that celebrated plurality and expressed apprehension about the political consequences, should intimacy "fuse" individuals and create classes, mobs, or masses instead of meaningful conversations. But we shall also see that Arendt stipulated conditions for conversations that corresponded with those favored by Augustine.[5]

Nonetheless, given her early aversion to the "unworldliness" of Augustine's ecclesial alternatives to late Roman politics and commerce, one could justifiably claim—in the awkward terms of this chapter's subheading—that Arendt decided "not to Augustine." We will attend to that claim shortly and make sense of it in light of her great admiration for the Founders of the American republic who proved to her that the public realm, in theory, could be a place of fair play and that officials respectful of others' opinions could rule humanely. Yet, during the 1950s and 1960s, her disenchantment seems to have inspired her return to Augustine. She witnessed the efforts of prominent American politicians to purge

---

[5]Arendt, *Denktagebuch: 1950–1973*, 2 vols., ed. Ursala Ludz and Ingeborg Nordmann, 2nd ed. (Munich: Piper), 2.525. For Augustine and "the worldlessness of charity, see Arendt, *The Human Condition*, 2nd ed. (Chicago: The University of Chicago Press, 1998), 53–54. Arendt's attitudes toward "the aversion of the intellectual elite" to the messy business of governing and its "yearning for anonymity" were admittedly ambivalent. She could applaud its resistance to "the radiant power of fame" and "the fascinating abnormal," to which the bourgeois as well as the mob succumbed, and she acquitted intellectuals who had been charged with having spawned justifications for totalitarian ideologies. But she also mentioned totalitarians' successful efforts to attract elites, and she could scold intellectuals for the "conviction" of many among them "that history . . . might as well be the playground of crackpots." Consult Arendt, *The Origins of Totalitarianism*, 2nd ed. (New York: Harcourt, 1968), 331–39.

dissident ideologies, noted the effect of white supremacists' racist rhetoric, and watched—dismayed—as rancor and deceit came to characterize public discourse. She tentatively construed what some scholars now call counterpublics as new beginnings, alongside of (and opposed to) political malpractice. And near the end of her career, she decided to revise and translate her doctoral dissertation into English, opting "to [and for] Augustine," whose alternatives (*neben und gegen*) were rather compatible with the alternative poleis to the large-canvas polis—the public realm—alternatives that Arendt was increasingly ready to risk advocating.[6]

Yet she never completely relinquished her suspicions about affections, suspicions that were most emphatically expressed in her criticisms of Jean Jacques Rousseau who consistently counted compassion as a political virtue. How unrealistic, Arendt complained. She understood Rousseau had predicated the possibility of compassion on what he presumed to be the goodness of human nature, which he inferred from corruption—much as one might infer crisp apples from the many rotten ones left in the orchards. Arendt mocked the logic. To her mind, the rot was so pervasive and corruption so contagious that one could not tell what had rotted. Nurture trumped whatever goodness nature possessed. Arendt, in effect, ushered Rousseau from the front to the back benches of political theory for having been naïve to trust affections to give public life a kinder, gentler texture.[7] She found Augustine to be more realistic, yet she considered goodness, as he and his colleagues in the churches conceived of it, equally problematic. Augustine—unlike Rousseau—thought human nature vile, powerless to renounce and resist evil until divine grace inspired faith and love. But that same grace informed as well as reformed the faithful, and its information (or infusion) compelled them to bear witness to a celestial good independent of political practice, to

---

[6]For "counterpublics," see Cristina Beltrán's adaptation of the term (borrowed from Michael Warner's *Publics and Counterpublics* [London: Zone Books, 2005]) in "Going Public: Hannah Arendt, Immigrant Action, and the Space of Appearance," *Political Theory* 37 (2009), 609. But Shin Chiba, "Hannah Arendt on Love and the Political: Love, Friendship, and Citizenship," *Review of Politics* 57 (1995), 506–12 contends that, "in later life," Arendt continued "exclud[ing] all forms of love as sentiment" from her meditations on political virtue. This chapter argues otherwise.
[7]Arendt, *On Revolution* (New York: Penguin, 1963), 70–71.

attest that "goodness [was] not only impossible within the confines of the public realm [but] destructive of it."[8] One could say, and this study has, that Augustine—and Agamben—looked to have the ways of this world "destroyed," though in disposition rather than "in deed." Augustine, however, struck Arendt as "very dangerous"; his twentieth-century heirs (unnamed in her work) unmasked what they took to be the decadence of this mortal world and boasted of their immortality; "these people," she insisted, must not be let "into politics."[9]

Arendt's warning is hard to reconcile with her contention that Augustine's "unworldly" worldview was "without any consequences for political philosophy."[10] In effect, she left us with two Augustines. One is irrelevant ("without any consequences"); the other, "very dangerous." It seems, though, that she shuttles between these two and, we shall discover, learned to incorporate both, coming to favor a pariah's perspective—as Augustine favored the pilgrim's perspective—to the preoccupations and perceptions of citizens in the terrestrial city. Conceivably, Arendt never became fully aware that Augustine's criticism of inauthenticity and arrogance in the public realm was rather consistent with hers—with her complaints about the political practices associated with her adopted republic as she came to despair of the disreputable desires behind lofty, state-of-the-art political sentiments in her time. But she did come extremely close to exonerating him for having excoriated late Roman political practice. Without denying the raft of repudiations that accompanied talk of virtue in Augustine's sermons, polemical treatises, and *City of God*, Arendt contrasted "the great sanity" of his response to early Christianity's deferred eschatological hopes

---

[8]Arendt, *The Human Condition*, 77; Arendt, "Understanding Politics," *Partisan Review* 20 (1953), 390.

[9]Arendt, "Arendt on Arendt," in *Hannah Arendt: The Recovery of the Public World*, ed. Melvyn A. Hill (New York: St. Martin's, 1979), 311.

[10]Arendt, *The Promise of Politics*, ed. Jerome Kohn (New York: Schocken, 2005), 59. Many of the political philosophers and historical theologians who would disagree (including this author)—and who disagree with each other—appear in Michael S. Bruno's useful survey, *Political Augustinianism: Modern Interpretations of Augustine's Political Thought* (Minneapolis: Fortress Press, 2013).

with the "horrible" hostility toward secular philosophy and politics of his fellow North African, Tertullian.[11]

The scholarly consensus keeps Arendt steadfastly dismissive of Augustine. If Stephan Kampowski is right, her mind was made up while she wrote her dissertation in 1929, suggesting Augustine opposed *caritas* (love and care) to *cupiditas* (acquisitiveness to the point of avarice). His sentiments may have seemed sane to her, but Kampowski alleges that she could never have thought them politically sound, because she believed Augustine instructed the faithful to orient *caritas* exclusively to their creator and redeemer. Such instruction "emptied [*caritas*] of material content." Eric Gregory agrees, and, if one reads only the dissertation and selective remarks in her subsequent work, Augustine's theocentricity, as Arendt interprets it, all but shreds the social relevance of *caritas*. Soteriological interests dwarfed ethical concerns. Neighbors became instruments or opportunities; "love of neighbor [was] merely an occasion to love God in the neighbor" and "finally transfers attention away from the neighbor to God."[12]

Freedoms and friendships Augustine associated with *caritas* appeared "negative" to Arendt, who showed little sympathy for his brooding about the propriety of wading into the shallows of diocesan and provincial politics that normally gave administrative effectiveness highest priority.[13] She grew excited, as we stated, about those deliberations that were unlike anything in the late Roman world, conferences during which "thoughtful and erudite Founders" of the American republic shaped its new government.[14] She was inspired by Thomas Jefferson's enthusiasm for discussions with his congressional colleagues. The tedium and tensions forgotten, Jefferson, to her mind, had written rhapsodically about "the joys of discourse, of legislation, and of transacting business—persuading and being persuaded," which, she claimed, "were to [him] no less conclusively a foretaste of an eternal bliss to come than the

---

[11] Arendt, *Human Condition*, 74.
[12] Stephan Kampowski, *Arendt, Augustine, and the New Beginning: The Action Theory and Moral Thought of Hannah Arendt in the Light of Her Dissertation on Augustine* (Grand Rapids: Eerdmans, 2008), 174–76, 201–2; Gregory, *Politics and the Order of Love*, 233–37.
[13] Arendt, *Denktagebuch*, 1:404-05.
[14] Arendt, *On Revolution*, 14.

delights of contemplation had been for medieval piety." The joys Augustine reserved for pilgrims apparently were available also to Jefferson's conferees.[15] Arendt believed they had cleverly crafted their governmental structure, providing incentives for an opposition party (preparing to govern) to cooperate as well as compete with a party in power. Conspicuous in her queue of to-dos, she told Karl Jaspers, was to explain the virtues of the American republican regime to Europeans.[16] Jefferson had seen the new regime as the Roman republic remodeled. Arendt could see the argument but was drawn to Thomas Paine's statement that "what Athens was in miniature, America will be in magnitude."[17]

Arendt's analysis, however, favored neither Rome nor Athens as the source of what she consistently evaluated as a heroic effort. Yet identifying the source led her to criticize the result. She traced Jefferson's "foretaste of eternal bliss" to what occurred earlier in town hall forums and regretted that the republic, once created, overshadowed the local assemblies in which friendships and reciprocities sustained collegial discourse. She regretted the failure to sustain the local discourses.[18] But, as long as the likes of Paine and Jefferson exhilarated her, Arendt placed Augustine among ne'er-do-wells. His political theory, she once scowled, simply recycled "pious banalities" that had originated with swarms of politically unschooled Platonists and that had no bearing on meaningful political action in the age of revolutions and renovations or in the polis-come-of-age in the twentieth century. Whenever Arendt was enamored of republican protocols and excited by the prospects for action and authenticity writ large in the public realm, as we noted, she decided not to Augustine.[19]

But, as her hopes to locate new beginnings on the large canvas of public life appeared unreasonable, she may have recalled the lesson one of her early protagonists, Rahel Varnhagen, learned in the late

---

[15] Arendt, *On Revolution*, 122–23.
[16] Arendt, *Briefwechsel*, 504.
[17] Arendt, *On Revolution*, 188.
[18] Arendt, *On Revolution*, 166–67. Richard King, *Arendt and America* (Chicago: University of Chicago, 2015), 226 rightly says that reading Arendt's admiration for Paine, Jefferson, and their colleagues "as an unalloyed celebration of the American founding" "would be a mistake."
[19] Arendt, *Promise of Politics*, 56.

eighteenth and early nineteenth centuries, a lesson reminiscent of Augustine's. Arendt's biography of Varnhagen, to which she turned soon after completing her dissertation on Augustine, recorded her subject's observation that patriotism ordinarily elapsed after crises had passed and the same putrid order returned.[20] Salon culture was part of Varnhagen's response. Her attic salons hosted the erudite who appreciated a place and time away from the political chaos of the Napoleonic era—for some in Berlin, no doubt, a place and time to forget the demoralizing consequences of Prussia's humiliation. The company and conversation did not amount to a full-scale retreat, yet Arendt—studying them, the Jewish woman who started the salon, and the salon's arguably parvenu aspirations to become part of the literary culture—encountered an alternative, creative, pariah counterculture. She would come to embrace the role of pariah, as Augustine would have had his parishioners play the part of pilgrims. She found statist solutions to social problems unattractive. Although she helped to raise and distribute funds for refugees in Palestine, she replied to a Zionist who anticipated her full-throated support for the state of Israel that she "never in my life 'loved' any people; the only kind of love I know and believe in," she added "is the love of persons."[21]

Disenchantment

We now know that Arendt's admiration for the Founders' recipes for an American republic was not uncritical. What they created was unsurpassed in many ways, but she was certain that their failure to reserve a special place and prerogatives for local assemblies, "the original springs of all political activity," led to the "wither[ing] away of the revolutionary spirit." Founders of the French republic, Saint Just and Robespierre, kept that spirit alive for a time by

---

[20] Arendt, *Rahel Varnhagen: Lebengeschichte einer deutschen Jüdin aus der Romantik* (Munich: Piper, 1959), 179: *alles wieder in die faule Ordnung kommt.*
[21] Arendt's letter to philosopher and historian Gershom Scholem is quoted in Daniel Maier-Katkin and Nathan Stoltzfuss, "Hannah Arendt on Trial," *The American Scholar* 82 (2013), 100. Also see Arendt, *Rahel Varnhagen*, 199–200 and Arendt, *The Jew as Pariah: Jewish Identity and Politics in the Modern Age*, ed. Ron H. Feldman (New York: Grove, 1978), 67–69.

promoting municipal club-like cohorts as "promising organs" of a new order. But their revolution ended badly; those "organs" became "instruments of terror."[22] Arendt noted that the larger poleis, which emerged after American and French revolutions, marginalized and sometimes suppressed smaller congresses and conferences where the fervor for popular participation in government had incubated. From the late 1950s, her observations of political practice and her studies of American political conundrums had already stirred her suspicion that the consent of the governed existed only in political oratory. It had "lost all plausibility" as bureaucrats deferred or abrogated citizen participation.[23]

The Founders anticipated that citizens' participation could cause trouble. James Madison assumed that multiple factions would keep any one of them from monopolizing discussions and from dictating policy to the detriment of the others. But Arendt saw the flaw in his reasoning as she watched from Europe during the late 1930s and into the 1940s while American isolationists controlled debate, shaped policy, and stymied efforts to draw the United States into the defense of rectitude and freedom.[24] Decades later, closer to events, she witnessed the interventionists in government and in the media lying to the American public and propelling the country into a war in Southeast Asia that became terribly unpopular. Her laments, historians now say, "anticipated the despair" that soon thereafter was "translated into the view that all politicians were corrupt."[25]

Arendt also complained that America's "revolutionary spirit" had atrophied. Insurgents ceded the capital to bureaucrats, and bureaucrats were slow to respond to moral crises. She told Karl

---

[22] Arendt, *On Revolution*, 231–35; Arendt, "Founding Fathers," Library of Congress, Arendt collection, 023441, section 3.

[23] Arendt, *Crises of the Republic* (New York: Harcourt, 1972), 88–89.

[24] Arendt, "Cui Bono," *Aufbau*, April 3, 1942, 3.

[25] For Arendt's "American jeremiad," consult, inter alia, Seyla Benhabib, *The Reluctant Modernism of Hannah Arendt* (London: Sage, 1996), 203–5; Mira L. Siegelberg, "Things Fall Apart: J. G. A. Pocock, Hannah Arendt, and the Politics of the Time," *Modern Intellectual History* 10 (2013), 120–24; Kei Hiruta, "An Anti-utopian Age: Isaiah Berlin's England, Hannah Arendt's America, and Utopian Thinking in Dark Times," *Journal of Political Ideologies* 22 (2017), 19–21; and for her thoughts on "the interconnectedness of deception and self-deception," Arendt, *Crises of the Republic*, especially, 34–43.

Jaspers that Washington seemed numb to—and, in the 1950s and early 1960s, ostensibly unaffected (*rührt sich nicht*) by—riotous, abhorrent reactions to court-ordered desegregation. Were Jefferson's and Paine's successors prepared to wait indefinitely for a comprehensive solution to their country's—her country's—problems to come from some other-than-political source.[26] Arendt started to look beyond the primary polis for new beginnings as she chronicled what she depicted as "the dismal failure" of revolutions in the twentieth century.[27]

She had intimate experience of one earlier failure. She was a teenager in Germany when proto-communists, the *Spartakusbund*, made arrestingly promising efforts to counter resurgent nationalism immediately after the First World War. But it proved impossible to turn the working classes into a fatherland. The *Bund* rapidly unraveled; its leaders were assassinated; communism became Bolshevism. Internationalism gave way to "insane nationalism," which, as Arendt looked on, torched Europe. Communists across the Atlantic were stumped. They could not fathom the worsening conditions over which Europe's authoritarian regimes presided until Stalin's non-aggression pact with Hitler in 1939 rattled them.[28]

But blame for ignorance and indifference, in Arendt's essays, usually rains down on bureaucrats, who were proficient at manipulating constituents' perceptions, affections, hopes, and fears. They undercounted casualties, suppressed "inconvenient facts," lay flimsy foundations beneath uncorroborated accounts of select events, exaggerating political or military gains. They seemed not to think that such "opinion manipulation" was bad form. Arendt trusted truth would out, but seldom in a timely fashion. The Pentagon Papers in 1971 revealed the lies that attended America's intervention in Vietnam; Nazis' frauds were disclosed after the collapse of the Third Reich; fictions perpetuated by the powerful tended to have long shelf lives.[29]

Lies and a granite resolve to defend them sustained regimes for a spell but, Arendt said, destroyed "the political," replacing it with

---

[26] Arendt, *Briefwechsel*, 607.
[27] Arendt, *Men in Dark Times* (London: Cape, 1970), 34–35, 42–43.
[28] Arendt, "Gestern waren sie noch Kommunisten," *Aufbau*, July 31, 1953, 19.
[29] Arendt, *Denktagebuch*, 2:629–31; Arendt, *Crises of the Republic*, 12–13.

something bureaucratic and, to her mind, definitely defective—
with something vertical, rather than meaningfully reciprocal and
horizontal.[30] Instead of promoting a plurality of perspectives,
public life and statist poleis channeled vitality into what Agamben
calls "forms of life," which bear some resemblance to what Arendt
classified as forms of labor that keep persons from re-purposing
themselves in conversations with others. Without markedly
distorting the thought of either, we might park Agamben's study
of biopolitics and his Foucauldian declaration that we live in "a
disciplinary universe" alongside Arendt's lament that "we live in
a civilization that threatens life."[31] Arendt identified that threat
with what she termed "society." For her, Margaret Canovan
remarks, without referring to Agamben, "society" favored "the
absorption of whole populations into forms of life." Society prized
conformity, not plurality and individuality. "The social" did not
encourage political discussion; it led to bureaucratization, and
bureaucrats were rewarded for "undeviatingly" carrying out their
"instructions from above." Adolf Eichmann, mindlessly following
orders to effect a final solution to the Nazis' "Jewish problem," was,
Arendt distastefully—though not dismissively—said, the "perfect
bureaucrat," "terribly and terrifyingly normal."[32]

Arendt's remedy for bureaucratization and for the invidious
influence of "the social," which set the conditions for the

---

[30]For a discussion of the "vertical" and "horizontal" dimension, see Jürgen Fohrmann, "Die Intervention der Stimme und die Kritik der 'Gedankenlosigkeit': Hannah Arendt in Gesellschaft," in *Hannah Arendt und Giorgio Agamben: Parallelen, Perspektiven, Kontroversen*, ed. Eve Geulen, Kai Kauffmann, and Georg Mein (Munich: Fink, 2008), 219–21.
[31]See Arendt, *Denktagebuch*, 2:714; Arendt, *Human Condition*, 139–44; and Agamben, *Signatura rerum: Sul metodo* (Turin: Bollati Boringhieri, 2008), 18–20.
[32]Arendt, *Eichmann in Jerusalem* (New York: Viking, 1963), 45–46, 137. Arendt's comment on Eichmann's terrifying normality is quoted in Nathaniel Popper, "A Conscious Pariah," *The Nation*, April 19, 2010, 30. Her critics accused her of enlisting Eichmann—on the strength of his plans to deport Jews—as a proto-Zionist, for which, see Arendt's response to Gershom Scholem, "Sie haben misverstanden," *Aufbau*, December 20, 1963, 17. Also see Margaret Canovan, *Hannah Arendt: A Reinterpretation of her Political Thought* (Cambridge: Cambridge University Press, 1992), 119–21 and, for an analysis of Arendt's distinctions between "the social" and "the political," see Hanna Fenichel Pitkin, *The Attack of the Blob: Hannah Arendt's Concept of the Social* (Chicago: The University of Chicago Press, 1998), 188–89.

bureaucratic domination of "the political" was a resurgence of respect for plurality and conversation. She looked forward to a new beginning, "a revival" of "the political," which she listed as one of the healing arts. Still, "the degradation" of political discourse and practice in her time increasingly troubled her.[33] From her first studies of totalitarianism, she sensed how weightless political virtues could seem to citizens chasing after an empire. Arendt's *Origins of Totalitarianism* recorded how and explained why the "giants of the imperialist enterprise" colonized the poleis of Europe before exporting money and militia to their advantage—and to the disadvantage of what persists as the underdeveloped world. She published her findings in 1951. They amounted to a comprehensive indictment of *cupiditas*, which bears a striking resemblance to the complaints that Augustine registered, complaints she chronicled in her dissertation. Arendt's *Origins* also associated *cupiditas* with the "lust for power" that animated leaders of fascist mobs, but, whereas previous generations of imperialists "dominat[ed] and terroriz[ed]" colonized others—extramurally, one might say—fascists improvised their "apparatus[es] of coercion" initially to dominate and terrorize "from within."[34]

Oddly, in one of her later essays, either Arendt forgot or ignored Augustine's forthright identification of *cupiditas* and the lust to dominate with Rome's territorial expansion. *Imperium* in the Mediterranean world "fell to" the Romans; it "was pressed upon them almost against their will," she pronounced, leaving that "almost" to vex or tantalize historians. She never undertook the legwork required to interrogate her principal source, Theodor Mommsen.[35] For her reading of Rome's reach was incidental, not central, to her analysis of totalitarian domination in her *Origins* which has been characterized as the "twentieth-century version of Augustine's *City of God*."[36] The reference seems justifiable. And, even if she continued to minimize republican and imperial Rome's craving for territory—as Augustine did not—she almost certainly

---

[33] Arendt, *Human Condition*, 22–24, 206–7.
[34] Arendt, *Origins of Totalitarianism*, 136–37, 325.
[35] Arendt, *The Promise of Politics*, 186–87.
[36] Joanna Vecchiarelli Scott, "A Detour through Pietism: Hannah Arendt on St Augustine's Philosophy of Freedom," *Polity* 20 (1988), 411–12.

had his explanation in mind when, two years after *Origins* appeared, she suggested that totalitarianism expressed "the lust for power and a will to dominate."[37] At the end of the decade, having witnessed sovereign powers in her adopted country conduct witch hunts and populist officials in its southernmost regions pander to prejudiced constituents, Arendt conceded that "goodness . . . as a consistent way of life is impossible within the confines of the public realm."[38]

She knew that impresarios of the public realm applied to unwanted others the very characterizations used to describe their improbity. Nazi propagandists, during the 1920s and 1930s, long before their regime devised its "final solution," denounced assimilated Jews for lusting after profit, power, and position after having betrayed Germany for financial advantage during the First World War.[39] The blame game persisted after the second. Despondent Germans, Arendt grimly reported, were as susceptible to the Nazis' lines on the lusts of others in 1947 as they had been when loyalty to Hitler and the National Socialists was rewarded with what must have seemed at the time to be an astounding series of successes.[40] She did discern one critical difference. Despair led many defeated Germans to see themselves as victims of their own lust for *Lebensraum*. But victorious Americans were blind to their lusts, which were stirred by prosperity (getting more and wanting more) and by what Arendt perceived as the dexterity of a feverishly active "entertainment industry"—rather than fed by unwelcome austerities. She wrote about the "gargantuan appetites" and the "crazy extravagance" that dulled Americans' wits. She thought that their "society, dazzled by the abundance of its growing fertility," could hardly be expected to comprehend its "futility."[41] They were convinced "that they really

---

[37]Arendt, "Understanding and Politics," *Partisan Review* 4 (1953), 381. Also, for discussions of domination in her journal, see Arendt, *Denktagebuch*, 1:367-68 and 2:619.
[38]Arendt, *Human Condition*, 77. Hans-Jörg Sigwart, *The Wandering Thought of Hannah Arendt* (New York: Palgrave Macmillan, 2015), 100–2 characterizes Arendt's "deviation or alienation from politics" as "gradual."
[39]Arendt, "Des Teufels Redekunst," *Aufbau*, May 8, 1942, 20.
[40]Arendt, *Briefwechsel*, 120.
[41]Arendt, *Human Condition*, 135. Compare Augustine, ep. 138.14. See Arendt, *Denktagebuch*, 1:445; Arendt, *Between Past and Future* (New York: Penguin, 1977), 203–4; and Arendt, "Society and Culture," *Daedalus* 89 (1960), 278–83, for the insatiable appetites.

had come to live in the best of all possible worlds." They withdrew from what the Founders of their republic created: a public forum where activism, free speech, and plurality might be celebrated. Instead, "the individual [had gotten] the better of the citizen."[42]

Arendt sized up the obsessions with consumption and regretted that they drove American citizens to give labor and productivity an "almost undisputed predominance." "The explosion of production and consumption," she alleged, had undesirable consequences and ought not to have been mistaken as "progress in the direction of freedom."[43] Dedication to production and to labor had all but swallowed up public life and sabotaged political practice. Arendt reserved the words "action" and "activity" for the latter two. When people meet as producers, she claimed, they do not meet as persons. They market their labor, and their primary concern is "with exchangeable commodities," a concern that, in her view, leads to a "lack of relatedness to others" and to "the increasing depersonalization of public and social life." Arraigning conformity, consumerism, and depersonalization, Arendt's indictments appear similar in some respects to complaints C. Wright Mills registered in the postwar period about "the ostracism of mind from public affairs."[44] But to attribute Arendt's disenchantment with the public realm to fellow authors—to Mills, who lectured nearby in New York City in the 1950s, or even to Augustine—unfairly discounts her observations of then current events. Her essays on deceit, discontent, and "dark times" show how headlines had eroded her confidence in the public realm—in *the* polis. Her exasperation showed in 1955: "why is it so hard to love this world?," she asked her journal.[45]

Alternative poleis: Natality and plurality

But might parts of the world be cleared of obsessions with production, and consumption? Could those zones be reserved

---

[42]Arendt, *On Revolution*, 131.
[43]Arendt, *Human Condition*, 128–29, Arendt, *Between Past and Future*, 247–49.
[44]Compare Arendt, *Human Condition*, 209–10, 243 with Mills, *The Power Elite*, 2nd ed., 357–59.
[45]Arendt, *Denktagebuch*, 1:522: *warum ist es so schwer die Welt zu lieben?*

for what Arendt considered meaningful political action? David Marshall questions whether we are right to think spatially. Despite her "interests in spatial and temporal compactness," Marshall maintains that Arendt conceived of her unconventional poleis as "congeries of controversial topoi around which debates accreted." Such "non-literal spaces" were free from "the tyranny of the here and now" and filled with "reactions" of long-dead others as well as contemporaries.[46] Yet Arendt generally required that immediacy and familiarity create a climate within a "where" in which rival perspectives could be shared and sifted—spaces or, as she once remarked, "oases" for thinking, speaking, and acting with others. All that, she trusted, would redeem politics from bureaucracy.[47] In practice, the participants' self-absorption was an obstacle. To scrub away self-interest and set aside the formalities to which political agents had been habituated would be no cakewalk. It required colossal effort, but it would be necessary to create what Arendt called "political space proper."[48] Jennifer Ring's appraisal appears accurate. Maintenance issues would keep cropping up and beset any impresario trying to "eliminate" from those spaces or oases "all party and governmental administrative apparatuses" to ensure free and "full voluntary participation."[49]

Agamben anticipated the problem, calling for strenuous combat against apparatuses that held subjects captive (*corpo a corpo coi dispositivi*).[50] Augustine concluded that captivity to the protocols and apparatuses of political culture in late antiquity was natural inasmuch as political practices derived from and amplified individuals' egocentrism. Although all were sinful and sin cast them down (*in imo jacet*), they insisted on raising themselves and

---

[46] David Marshall, "The Polis and its Analogues in the Thought of Hannah Arendt," *Modern Intellectual History* 7 (2010), especially 132–33, 145–48.

[47] Arendt, "Einfuhrung in die Politik II," in *Hannah Arendt: Was ist Politik, Fragmente aus dem Nachlass*, ed. Ursula Ludz (Munich: Piper, 1993), 96–97. For "oases," see Arendt, *Promise of Politics*, 202–3, but also note Arendt, *On Revolution*, 267–68, where the metaphor is used quite differently to refer to elites embedded within political apparatuses rather than to counterpublics somehow shielded from "what went wrong with politics."

[48] Arendt, *On Revolution*, 21.

[49] Jennifer Ring, "The Pariah as Hero: Hannah Arendt's Political Actor," *Political Theory* 19 (1991), 448.

[50] Agamben, *Che cos'è un dispositivo*, 26, 29, and 32.

ignored the help on offer from God. Augustine repeatedly explained to them that they had to accept God's grace to rise above their predicaments.[51] He turned this imperative into a constant refrain even before the Pelagians crossed to Africa. He repeatedly contrasted self-reliance with humility, as we know, and he demanded that the faithful confess their inadequacies, surrender their Goliath-sized self-esteem, gratefully receive God's grace, and exhibit the humility and repentance King David's psalms elegantly expressed.[52]

Unlike Augustine, who stressed the need for divine assistance and unlike Agamben, who would have had refugees initiate and complete intrapsychic struggles against convention more or less unaided, Arendt prescribed interpersonal deliverance. Her study of early modern salons gave her a glimpse of redemptive sociability.[53] "Disparate kinds of councils" tremendously impressed her, though she regretted that "central power" eventually "deprive[d such] constituent bodies of their original power to constitute." Power too soon became "the property of . . . rulers" of larger entities and the bureaucrats they appointed to administer them.[54] Arendt flirted with making the deliberations in the Athenian agora a model for a time but despaired, as Agamben does, that its appeal would be quite limited. Marketplaces and media too effectively commodify persons and depersonalize transactions. Arendt settled for a generalization; retaining her faith that "suitable organization[s] of the people" may "arise out of acting and speaking together," she specified the social and atmospheric conditions conducive to the creation of poleis where communities "find [their] proper location[s] almost any time and anywhere" persons assert and preserve each other's dignity—anytime and anywhere they "exist not merely like other living and animate things but make their appearance explicitly."[55]

For Augustine, persons emerged "explicitly" from struggles with sin; for Agamben, they did so after battling social conditioning. For Arendt, "explicitly" appears to suggest that persons emerge

---

[51] Augustine, *Io ev. tr.* 22.15.
[52] See, for example, Augustine, s. 32.9-10.
[53] Arendt, *Rahel Varnhagen*, 63.
[54] Arendt, *On Revolution*, 227–29; 258–59.
[55] Arendt, *Human Condition*, 198–99. Also see John Douglas Macready, "Hannah Arendt and the Meaning of Human Dignity," *Journal of Social Philosophy* 47 (2016), 411–12.

ready to make new beginnings and contribute to conversations. Hence, in her universe, explicit emergence was social. Privacy, per se, was unobjectionable, but Arendt contended that privacy made scant contribution to meaningful political actions—quite understandably—but also to subjects' realistic self-assessments. In the first of three essays in her final ruminations on *The Life of the Mind*, she took issue with Descartes, for whom, she averred, thinkers' sense of self (and of reality) were "guaranteed" by those thinkers thinking in solitude. She had reservations. Thinkers do not appear "explicitly," she claimed, unless their thoughts "are made manifest to others." So thinking straight, self-disclosure, and generative political discourse depended on "perceiving and being perceived" simultaneously, which was, she said, "determinative of the polis." And one's political freedom, Arendt added elsewhere, depended "on the presence of others and on our being confronted with their opinions."[56]

We shall have more to say about "the presence of others," when we discuss what Arendt wrote at length about plurality, but it suffices now to suggest how important immediacy was to her. There could be no "*inter-est*" without it, and Arendt required "*inter-est*, which lies between people[,] . . . bind[s] them together," and gives "agent-revealing capacity" to "the web of human relations." Yet "*inter-est*" could only occur, if the poleis made room for and encouraged persons "acting and speaking directly *to* one another."[57] Arendt criticized Marxism for having attributed a spectacular solidarity to "masses," as if masses' movements were self-sustaining, and for settling eventually with Stalin, settling for ruthless statist solutions.[58] As we just noted, Arendt was suspicious of statist solutions. She distanced herself from her friends' Zionist extremism as early as the 1940s and, later, Judith Shklar notices, she was quarreling "with all sides of the American Zionist movement."[59] Simply put, Arendt was

---

[56] Arendt, *The Life of the Mind: Thinking* (New York: Harcourt Brace Jovanovich, 1970), 19–21; Arendt, *Promise of Politics*, 126–28.
[57] Arendt, *Human Condition*, 182–84 (emphasis in the original).
[58] Arendt, *Denktagebuch*, 1:392; Arendt, *Origins of Totalitarianism*, 319–20.
[59] Judith N. Shklar, "Hannah Arendt as Pariah," in *Political Thought and Political Thinkers*, ed. Stanley Hoffman (Chicago: The University of Chicago Press, 1998), 364–67 nonetheless, and surprisingly, terms Arendt "an ardent Zionist." For Arendt and Zionist extremism in Europe, see her "Ein erster Schrift," *Aufbau*, June 30, 1942, 15–16.

not a party partisan. As Eli Zaretsky argues, she should "in no way ... be assimilated to the social democratic traditions" because she took more seriously than most progressives "the uniquely personal" and interpersonal. In the final decades of her career, moreover, she was no more a meliorist with regard to the public realm than Augustine had been and Agamben is. She knew renovation in the public realm was greatly needed, yet she intimated as early as the 1950s that innovation and new beginnings in what Zaretsky calls "other spheres of life" would have a greater likelihood of success promoting forgiveness, familiarity, and genuine respect—all of which was absolutely necessary for new political *inter-ests*.[60]

"Every new beginning is by nature a miracle when seen and experienced from the standpoint of the processes it necessarily interrupts." The miraculous in Arendt's statement suggests that she had at hand vials of holy oil to anoint her new beginnings and award them transcendent importance. Her subjects are "miracle worker[s]" who beat the "overwhelming" "odds in favor of tomorrow unfolding just like today."[61] In her extended essay on *The Human Condition*, she classified "the miracle" as "a second birth" of the miracle worker—as an action "not forced upon us by necessity, like labor . . . not prompted by utility." Agamben refers to a similar sort of rebirth that occurs when "messianic" or "kairotic" time interrupts linear time to awaken subjects to their potential and to drain sovereign powers' protocols and laws of their significance. Arendt's new beginnings are not nearly as subversive, though Agamben would surely find nothing disagreeable in her applications of Augustine's reflections on beginning anew—on what she called "natality," applications asserting that to be "a beginner" is to "insert" oneself and "explicitly" become an "interruption."[62]

---

[60]See Arendt, *Human Condition*, 240–43 and Eli Zaretsky, "Hannah Arendt and the Meaning of the Public/Private Distinction," in *Hannah Arendt and the Meaning of Politics*, ed. Craig Calhoun and John McGowan (Minneapolis: University of Minnesota Press, 1997), 227.

[61]Arendt, *Promise of Politics*, 111–13.

[62]See Arendt, *Human Condition*, 176–77; Agamben, "Il Messia e il sovrano," 18; and Tyson Edward Lewis, "The Architecture of Potentiality: Weak Utopianism and Educational Space in the Work of Giorgio Agamben," *Utopian Studies* 23 (2012), 359.

Elisabeth Young-Bruehl, Arendt's discerning biographer, dates her subject's "concern for natality"—for new beginnings—to the late 1920s when she was preparing her doctoral dissertation and studying with Heidegger as well as Jaspers. That concern "was later brought urgently to the center of her thought by political experiences"—by Arendt's disenchantment.[63] Before then, she chronicled Rahel Varnhagen's fascination with Johann Gottlieb Fichte and with the confidence expressed in his early nineteenth-century lectures predicting that a fresh start was forthcoming. Despite deafening sounds of the wars in 1806, Varnhagen heard him tell countrymen to become *Samenkorn*, the seeds of an imposing German recovery. Yet she was a Jew, one among a partly assimilated but mostly pariah people, so, as inspired as she was by Fichte, Varnhagen's new beginnings germinated apart from the civic order he hoped to renew. From one vantage, her salons may seem to have been "places of attempted minority assimilation," as Richard King surmises, for "the exotic" mixed with "high society" there. As Arendt presents that "there," however, it was a new beginning; with what she called the pride of a pariah (*Hochmut des Paria*), Varnhagen created a space where cultured women and men of all confessions could gather. Arendt admired the achievement. Yet, in the 1930s, as she composed her *Varnhagen*—and despite the horrific choices forced on Jews—she was unprepared to let mistreatment of her family and friends scuttle the prospect that new beginnings might humanize civic order in the twentieth century.[64]

That prospect colored some of Arendt's later studies. Her reflections on the American Revolution, which we have already visited, extolled "the speech-making and decision-taking" that led to "the foundation of a new body politic" characterized by the Founders' "eagerness to . . . build a new house" on a new continent where "freedom can dwell." She took the early American republic as a specimen of humans' "faculty to begin something new," yet she

---

[63] Elisabeth Young-Bruehl, *Hannah Arendt: For Love of the World*, 2nd ed. (New Haven: Yale University Press, 2004), 495.
[64] Arendt, *Rahel Varnhagen*, 125–27. For Fichte's *Samenkorn einer . . . Nachkommenschafte*, see his *Reden an die deutsche Nation* (Hamburg: Felix Meiner, 1955), 179–81. For "minority assimilation," Richard H. King, "Hannah Arendt and the Uses of Literature," *Raritan* 36 (2017), 113.

admitted that it had failed. The capacity for novelty—as channeled through the revolutionary spirit—was attended by "an enormous pathos": insurgents' reach exceeded their grasp; their descendants ceased reaching. Arendt's term "pathos" could be read as a passion inspired by the desire to interrupt a history that fed (and was fed by) creatures' lust to dominate. But "pathos" could also refer to disappointments that followed as Americans realized their failure and to the disenchantment of Arendt and others discussing those disappointments.[65]

By 1953, what Arendt called "political data" persuaded her that "the central position the concept of beginning . . . must have in all political thought ha[d] been lost." Although she knew historical comparisons were untrustworthy (because history was usually written by uncharitable winners who were eager narratively to detonate charges against losers), she nonetheless ventured to compare her times with Augustine's. The latter, she gauged, were more like the former "than [like] any other [times] in recorded history." Augustine wrote his *City* "under the full impact of a catastrophic end . . . perhaps resembl[ing] the end to which we have come," she went on, adding that empires and populations in search of glory had taken terrible turns in both late antiquity and the twentieth century. The "turn" she witnessed, we now know, discouraged her and made it hard for humans to "reaffirm" their "capacity for beginning." "Moral commandments were no longer thought to be self-evident." She recalled that Nietzsche saw as much in his time and set out to find replacements for the "highflown phrases" and tiresome "preachings about the existence of conscience, which speaks with an identical voice to all." What Nietzsche found, however, was insufficient for Arendt, who regretted "that the only standard he came up with was Life itself." One can imagine her similarly assessing Agamben's efforts to liberate captive life and to alert captives to their unperceived potential; nonetheless, she understood that the reaffirmation of

---

[65]Arendt, *On Revolution*, 24–25. But compare Michael North, *Novelty: A History of the New* (Chicago: The University of Chicago Press, 2013), 17–18, which proposes that the pathos might follow from a rather recondite simultaneity between realization and disappointment, whereby "the new, as an ideal, is . . . ruined as soon as it is realized."

a "capacity for beginning" would be a "strange enterprise" that was unlikely to follow predictable, unambiguous courses. She and Agamben, therefore, would almost certainly have agreed that new beginnings were, in effect, eruptions of novelty and interruptions. Beginnings enacted beginners' estrangement from their times, as Augustine's pilgrims' progress enacted and attested their alienation, their "decathect" from conventional political protocols.[66]

Yet Arendt frequently hesitated. Two years before she compared the twentieth century with late antiquity, she confided that "the alien [was] a frightening symbol." In her *Origins of Totalitarianism*, she insinuated that alienation might undermine initiative and incapacitate change agents. She suggested citizens were better positioned to contribute to "common and coordinated effort[s]" to advance civilization. But by the end of that decade, comparisons she drew between Augustine's sense of catastrophe and her own had substantial bearing on *her* reaffirmation of what she enthusiastically described as humans' "faculty for interrupting" "the normal" and "natural" "course of nature and institutions" as well as on the development of a doctrine of natality.[67]

But Arendt does not appear to have expected the interruptions she commended to play out dramatically in the public realm. She acknowledged that her new beginnings would neither lead to nor end exquisitely with the "disappearance of . . . domination."[68] Hans-Jörg Sigwart is certain that, as her career developed, Arendt acknowledged that "the purpose of political action" was "not directly to engage and actively participate in politics, but to engage in critique."[69] She had confided to David Riesman that citizens who invest too much faith in political revivals and renovations become easy prey for Marxist and fascists.[70] If Eli Zaretsky is right, as

---

[66]Arendt, "Understanding and Politics," 390–91. For Arendt's mistrust of history, consult Annette Vowinckel, *Geschichtsbegriff und historisches Denken bei Hannah Arendt* (Cologne: Böhlau, 2001), 112–15. For Arendt's comments on Nietzsche, see her "Some Questions of Moral Philosophy," *Social Research* 61 (1994), 740–41.
[67]Compare Arendt, *Origins of Totalitarianism*, 301–2 with Arendt, *Human Condition*, 246–47.
[68]Arendt, *Promise of Politics*, 77–78.
[69]Sigwart, *Wandering Thought*, 127–28.
[70]See Arendt's letter to David Riesman, May 21, 1948, Library of Congress, Arendt Collection, 009235, 1.

early as the 1950s, Arendt's work came also to be understood as a critique of—and, arguably, the desecration of—"social democracy and the twentieth-century liberalism affected by it."[71] This is a rather big "if," but her doctrine of natality has something of a subversive, cutting edge and appears to be as much a refusal to capitulate to protocols that define political success as Agamben's resistance to biopolitically fashioned "forms of life" and Augustine's criticisms of the commonly accepted definitions of glory in late antiquity. Some recent literature plumping for radical innovation in education pairs Arendt and Agamben, celebrating the subversive implications of their offerings and opting for interruptions that challenge "trusted explanations" for the ways young citizens in the United States are taught. Mar Rosàs Tosas recruits both Arendt and Agamben to argue that "the goal of education should not be to help students insert themselves into their biocapitalistic world but to provide them with the chance to escape from its logic." James Magrini, principally interested in Arendt, finds her emphasis on natality creatively disruptive and agrees with Rosàs Tosas that new beginnings in education can only become influential once educators' common equations of authenticity with efficiency and closure are denounced.[72] Augustine would have supplied and amplified God's part in the subversion, yet our previous remarks on his lessons imparted to catechumens could be docked alongside those Rosàs Tosas and Magrini extract from their sources.

It is tempting to associate Arendt's advocacy of natality (and, as we shall see, plurality) with seminars that liberate participants to engage in what she prized as "argumentative speech." She also identified compassion with an "intensity of listening" but wrote as if feelings of fondness jeopardized "the drawn-out wearisome processes of persuasion, negotiation, and compromise" she believed critical to political practice. Arendt could make compassion seem pernicious, as if it lifted "burdens of proof," the full weight of

---

[71] Zaretsky, "Hannah Arendt," 214.
[72] James M. Magrini, "An Ontological Notion of Learning Inspired by the Philosophy of Hannah Arendt: The Miracle of Natality," *Review of Contemporary Philosophy* 12 (2013), 83–84 and Mar Rosàs Tosas, "Educational Leadership Reconsidered: Arendt, Agamben, and Bauman," *Studies in Philosophy and Education* 35 (2016), 359.

which had to be felt if persons were to converse productively.[73] Yet compassion occasionally made comebacks when Arendt introduced her thoughts on the importance of plurality and tolerance, depicting them as the *sine quibus non* of successful new beginnings, she seemed to recognize the part compassion played maintaining friendships. Without fondness, "the surrounding presence of others"—each person's "constant contact with the web of [others'] acts and words"—could hardly have constituted poleis committed to the freedoms of participants and their pursuits of truths.[74]

To be sure, Arendt never wholly relinquished positions she formulated in her doctoral dissertation. Augustine's otherworldliness was an obstacle; he would have made the world an inhospitable wilderness, she claimed, despite its status as his God's creation.[75] What he valued, however, appealed to her. Forgiveness, friendships, and their accessory affections had their place, as Jon Nixon documents; they created interconnections without jeopardizing the "*inter-ests*" she so prized or silencing "argumentative speech."[76] Hence, Augustine became far less an obstacle to plurality than did political polarization or the ecstatic conformity totalitarian regimes inspired. When polarization prevailed, as, in Arendt's view, it often did, opinion mattered more than truth. And opinions sometimes slithered to extremes. Whoever looked to tell the truth in the public forum (*im politischen Raum*), she told her journal in 1963, must expect to be confronted by interlocutors wanting only to hear whether the "truth" on offer corroborated or contradicted their opinions. Polarization was problem enough, yet what frequently emerged from any clash between opinions, Arendt explained, was worse: fraud masquerading as ideology and fanatically thrust forward by mobs. Their modus vivendi was violence, which

---

[73]Arendt, *On Revolution*, 76–77.

[74]Arendt, *Human Condition*, 188.

[75]Arendt, *Liebesbegriff*, 13: *in der caritas lebend wird die Welt zur Wüste, statt zur Heimat*. And, for Arendt's dissent, see Gaetano Rametta, "Osservazioni su *Der Liebesbegriff bei Augustin* di Hannah Arendt," in *La pluralità irrappresentabile: Il pensiero politico di Hannah Arendt*, ed. Roberto Esposito (Naples: QuattroVenti, 1987), 126–29.

[76]Jon Nixon, *Hannah Arendt and the Politics of Friendship* (London: Bloomsbury, 2015), 38.

obliterated all possibilities for what she defined as political action and speech. Friendships were friendlier to both.[77]

The objective Arendt associated with both was "the testing that arises from contact with other people's thinking," testing of one's own thoughts alongside or against those of others and testing the thoughts of others as well. No single systematic approach was commended. Lectures on Kant that she was revising when she died in 1975 recommended "the art of critical thought," suggesting that it could be developed more or less spontaneously. But she warned that, should it became a lost art, political discourse would come undone and progressive political action would cease and desist. Should it be practiced and refined, Arendt predicted excellent results in poleis: the predominance and popularity of what she termed "impartiality." She clarified by stipulating that she was not countenancing the sort of impartiality keeping practitioners "altogether above the melée" and passing as objectivity. She was referring to an impartiality that encouraged the "enlargement" of perspective, which, she advised, would come from engagements with plural prejudices. Success, measured by "enlarged" perspectives and impartial speakers and agents, would come to those willing to make new beginnings.[78]

Among practitioners of impartiality and the art of critical thought, three Greeks particularly impressed Arendt. Homer was fair-minded in hymns praising both Hector and Achilles. Not only did Homeric "history" "leave behind the common interest in [the Greeks'] side"; it "discards the alternative of victory or defeat." Herodotus and Thucydides were equally and, in Arendt's judgment, exceptionally impartial. Seductive as it might be to think of them as solo celebrities, she linked their ability "to look upon the same world from" others' standpoints, "to see the same in very different and frequently opposing aspects" to their "long experience in polis-life" with the "inexhaustible flow of arguments" in Athens.[79]

---

[77]Arendt, *Denktagebuch*, 2:621: *Wer die Wahrheit sagen will, ist konfrontiert mit Leuten, die sagen: Drücke dich nicht, bist du für oder gegen uns? Zwei Lügen*. For the differences between mobs and masses in Arendt's thinking, consult Vowinkel, *Geschichtsbegriff*, 97–98.
[78]Arendt, *Lectures on Kant's Political Philosophy*, ed. Ronald Beiner (Chicago: The University of Chicago Press, 1982), 42–43.
[79]Arendt, *Between Past and Future*, 51.

Arendt was saddened by moderns' inability to sustain a similar flow in the public forum. To those obstacles to plurality and natality we have already mentioned—ecstatic conformity and polarization—she added another, insinuating that it was a peculiarly modern form of conformity, caused by complacency rather than by authoritarian regimes' manipulation of opinions. Arendt thought complacency and conformity especially insidious during the 1950s in the United States. Instead of growing aware of itself as an increasingly pluralistic society, the country buttoned up against the winds of change. She fretted that "social conformism" was "becom[ing] an absolute—and a substitute for national homogeneity."[80] As we discovered, she attributed apathy to a sense of well-being and grieved that the citizens ceded political rights and responsibilities, not because they had been bullied but rather because they were flourishing and self-satisfied.[81] Democracy had become oligarchy, and oligarchs looked to bureaucrats to carry out orders. Fixed opinions that brought elites into councils tended to make "argumentative speech" acrimonious. While indifferent others abstained, therefore, power trumped truth, and intimidation counted as persuasion. Power and intimidation ruined republics.[82]

Where did that leave Arendt? And where does she lead us? Although disenchanted with political cultures in the public realm, her enthusiasm for plurality and natality was undiminished. In the late 1960s, serving on a jury in New York City, she enjoyed sifting differences of opinion. Apparently members of her panel gave free rein to their perceptions of the evidence presented or of the litigants' contested claims without allowing the contention in either the courtroom or jury room make their discussions unpleasant. Arendt told Karl Jaspers that those deliberations were invigorating.[83] Yet it would take something more enduring, as Liisi Keedus rightly

---

[80] Arendt, "Reflections on Little Rock," *Dissent* 6 (1959), 51. The controversial article argued that discrimination be "confined within the social sphere"—rather than doused completely—and kept from the political. Arendt's reflections ignited controversy, for which, see, inter alia, Daniel Cole, "A Defense of Hannah Arendt's Reflections on Little Rock," *Philosophical Topics* 39 (2011), 36–37.
[81] See Arendt's letter to Riesman, Arendt Papers, Library of Congress, 009240-41.
[82] Arendt, *Denktagebuch*, 1:439 (*Wo Gewalt ist, gibt es keine res publica*); also see *Denktagebuch*, 2:631.
[83] Arendt, *Briefwechsel*, 2:700–01.

suspects, to satisfy Arendt's hunger for "the specificity of political experience." To be sure, distillations of political experience in political philosophy were food for thought. They were a theorist's feast, but, Keedus continues, "to reach the real presence of others" and turn plurality to advantage, Arendt looked for poleis where participation (as action and speech) "open[ned] a world and ground[ed] community in an act of beginning."[84]

For explicit statements of the importance of "the real presence of others," Arendt could have turned to passages in Augustine's *City*, particularly the nineteenth book where pilgrims in public service were urged to be consoled by each other's love.[85] But Arendt only returned to her dissertation on Augustine's concept of love when she was contemplating retirement. His *City of God* does not appear to have come to mind while she prowled for alternative poleis, *neben und gegen*. The closest she came—and came often—to finding alternative consolations as she wrote about the ruin of the republic and the reach of bureaucracy—as well as about the public realm's failure to promote plurality, cultivate impartiality, and sustain new beginnings—was the company of colleagues and students she enjoyed while lecturing, from the 1950s, at a number of premiere American colleges and universities.

She distanced herself from what she took to have been Plato's objective: the academy ruling the polis. She preferred to think of the former as an "oasis," "an institutionalized space [reserved] for freedom," *neben und gegen*, opposing the "mendacious opinions and deceptive speech" of "the marketplace." Rather than trying to "mold politics," the academy, she argued, should represent a "turning away," "an *a-politia*."[86] Campus protests in the 1960s distressed her, yet she looks to have been allergic to the consensus among colleagues holding students ("young rebels") responsible. She was most disconcerted by what she called "the politicization" of higher education which followed when governments yoked

---

[84]Liisi Keedus, *The Crisis of German Historicism: The Early Political Thought of Hannah Arendt and Leo Strauss* (Cambridge: Cambridge University Press, 2015), 175–76.
[85]See, for example, Augustine, *civ.* 19.8: *mutua dilectio verorum et bonorum amicorum.... Qua ingenti malorum plena est terra.*
[86]Arendt, *Promise of Politics*, 133.

research and education to nefarious political purposes. She saw that as a "betrayal," "rightly [to be] deplored" by all who cherished the pursuit of truth.[87]

So, if college officials proved insufficiently agile to avoid corrosive political influences and thus to quiet their campus protests, where was Arendt likely to find a place for natality and plurality? Those two conditions must have seemed unsustainable to her on many occasions, not only in the public realm but also in any conceivable alternative polis. Certainly, prospects on a large canvas looked bleak, at best. Perhaps she came, at some unspecifiable time, to see that the only recourse was to work "to keep the public domain full of multiple ideas," as Ronald Arnett presumes, in effect, lowering Arendt's horizon of expectations. The location and support of the poleis "contributing to difference in the public domain," Arnett supposes, appeared a reasonable alternative to restructuring or renovating that domain.[88] And we now know that she would have wanted those poleis to contribute criticism as well as diversity—criticism of homogenization and polarization. So might it be fair to say that Arendt did not give up hoping for the sustainability of alternative poleis committed to plurality and new beginnings? Yet, because she was dismayed by seemingly, staggeringly pervasive temptations to conform and—in tension—tendencies to combat and polarize, she reserved a central place for forgiveness when advocating "a new politics" for a polis that, falling short of her loftiest expectations, might nonetheless retain the wherewithal for periodic renewals.

Forgiveness, she explained, "is the only reaction which does not merely re-act but acts anew."[89] Forgiveness "draw[s] . . . a line under past events . . . enabling people to make a new start in their relations with one another," Margaret Canovan explains, filing that "line" with the other evidence she accumulates to persuade colleagues "to abandon the conventional picture of Arendt judging modern politics in the light of a[n] . . . unambiguous theory of action,"

---

[87] Arendt, *Crises of the Republic*, 118–19, 189–90.
[88] Ronald C. Arnett, *Communication Ethics in Dark Times: Hannah Arendt's Rhetoric of Warning and Hope* (Carbondale: Southern Illinois University Press, 2012), 183–84.
[89] Arendt, *Human Condition*, 240–41.

which she supposedly "derived from an idealization of Athens" and from authors influenced by its political practice.[90] In theory, the centrality of forgiveness in Arendt's alternatives to prevailing poleis ought to ensure that "argumentative speech" did not lead to disruptions that made plurality repellant and conformity appealing. She wanted to "arrest tendencies towards large-scale conformism," Brian Singer says, but also to avoid heated competitions born of envy and insecurities, which refuse to die.[91]

Preparing her doctoral dissertation, Arendt would often have come across Augustine preaching forgiveness. His sermons suggest that he could not abide his parishioners' cavalier attitudes toward the magnitude of God's pardon and their ignorance of the obligations that it placed upon them to forgive others. Unless they stopped exonerating themselves and started to pardon others, they would never come to understand the importance of their messiah's mission, passion, and atonement. Temptations to boast of their virtues (*inflare se*) would overcome them, as, in Augustine's estimation, it overcame the Manichaean elite, the Pelagians, and most pagans. When, trespassed against, they craved vengeance, the faithful signaled that they cared more for their glory than for their God's.[92] Maybe Arendt also caught Augustine addressing magistrates, who presumed forgiveness was incompatible with political discipline, and reminding them that Cicero countenanced forgetting offenses.[93]

But the two knew forgiveness was rare among political rivals. Augustine's solace was what Daniel Burns depicts as an "inevitable" divergence between pilgrims' congregations and politicians' conferences.[94] One need not guess whether—only how often—the divergence that Augustine perceived seemed wide and inevitable to Arendt. She knew that, for him, pilgrims' (and for her, pariahs') lives must "unfold within society," yet she also knew he preferred that pilgrims enjoy "freedom from politics." She maintained that Augustine was responsible for "seculariz[ing] Christians' flight

---

[90]Canovan, *Hannah Arendt*, 138–39.
[91]Brian C. J. Singer, "Thinking Friendship With and Against Hannah Arendt," *Critical Horizons* 18 (2017), 11.
[92]Augustine, *en. Ps.* 111.4; Augustine, s. 58.6-7 (*inflare se*) and s. 114a.5.
[93]Augustine, ep. 138.9.
[94]Burns, "Augustine on the Moral Significance of Human Law," 297–98.

into seclusion, to a point where the faithful constituted within the world a totally new, religiously defined public space"—a zone that, "though public," "was not political."[95] But when Arendt referred to his strategy, perhaps the superiority of a life engaged in what is ordinarily seen as political practice seemed as specious to her as it had to him. Perhaps, revisiting his complaints about political culture, Arendt, as John McGowan says, "envision[ed] an excessive . . . binding of humans together by acts of promising and forgiving that sacrifice almost everything (including security and property) for the sake of relatedness."[96]

Citizens

Citizenship since the age of absolutism has been about security, property, and—often—some level of political participation for some. Political theorists variably assess how the demands placed on regimes to preserve their sovereignty affect their definitions of citizenship. Agamben's essays regularly argue that sovereign powers' self-interest spurs regimes to reconfigure religious rituals and acclamations and to use them to overawe citizens, so much so that divine or "eternal government" seems to have become the paradigm for modern political practices.[97] Meaningful popular participation is negligible; manipulation is widespread. Citizens conform worshipfully, accommodating what John Lechte and Saul Newman describe as "the dominance of the Same" and "the imperialism of the Same," whereby security and property are secured at the cost of dignity. Even more problematic—for Agamben, Arendt, and Augustine—governments (or, to include the sets of quasi-political executors of reigning regimes' policies, governmentality) excessively rely upon discipline to ward off dissent.[98]

---

[95] Arendt, *Promise of Politics*, 139.
[96] John McGowan, "Must Politics be Violent? Arendt's Utopian Vision," in *Hannah Arendt and the Meaning of Politics*, ed. McGowan and Craig Calhoun (Minneapolis: University of Minnesota Press, 1997), 285, as the title indicates considers Arendt's "vision" as utopian and "even foolhardy."
[97] Agamben, *Il Regno e la Gloria*, 181.
[98] See Vincent Lloyd, "A Critical Introduction to *The Kingdom and the Glory*," *Political Theology* 14 (2013), 59–62 and John Lechte and Saul Newman, *Agamben*

For Agamben, sovereign powers dictate forms of life that suppress citizens' potential to improvise a form of life expressive of their vitality. And because he is wary of prescriptions for this improvisation—because, as Catherine Mills elaborates, he wants to inspire "life lived in the experience of its own unity, its own potentiality"—Agamben leaves the messianic community, which should help "overturn being's expropriation by" sovereign powers and their spectacles, understipulated.[99] Indeed, his terminology has what Eva Geulen astutely calls a wide-ranging allusiveness (*ein grosser Anspielungshorizont*). "Form of life," as she suggests, is "riddling"; it invites multiple and sometimes conspicuously contrary or warring interpretations. But charges that the ambiguity of his remedies for captivity amount to anarchy are unfair.[100] Enunciating their degradation, pariahs shape what he depicts as a remnant, and his volume on Auschwitz closes with an archive, a collection of testimonials to the unspeakable, situating witnesses in a conversation, which, in effect, opposes oppression.[101] But such collections and conversations, strictly speaking, are not communities. If one stretches a bit to couple Arendt, from the 1950s, with Augustine—as kindred spirits endeavoring to lay the groundwork for alternative poleis—one undeniably strains to put Agamben with them, on this count. Nonetheless, if we make opposition to entrapment the distinctive feature of an alternative polity, Agamben's alternatives orbit with the other two. With them, he looks to undermine concepts of citizenship they construe as maintenance strategies that brace sovereign powers' pretensions.

To Agamben, citizenship amounts to acquiescence to captivity. Declarations of rights enfranchise citizens, to some extent, but they then swarm into "forms of life" (consumers, clients, or voyeurs) that, he alleges, "inscrib[e] them" into the states' (and statists')

---

and the Politics of Human Rights: Statelessness, Images, Violence (Edinburgh: Edinburgh University Press, 2013), 184–85.

[99]Catherine Mills, "Agamben's Messianic Politics: Biopolitics, Abandonment, and Happy Life," *Contretemps* 5 (2004), 52.

[100]Eva Geulen, "Wirklichkeit, Möglichkeiten, und Unmöglichkeiten: Zum Problem der Lebesnform bei Giorgio Agamben und Theodor Adorno," *MLN* 125 (2010), 644–45.

[101]Agamben, *Quel che resta di Auschwitz*, 133–36, 151–60.

commercial and juridico-political orders.[102] Arendt alluded to a similar entrapment when she wrote about citizens who dutifully "coordinated themselves" to the routines and roles sanctioned by sovereign powers. Citizens became impassive. Even the coordination required little exertion. Much as in the Germany she fled in the 1930s, poleis decades later countenanced and encouraged careless conformity. She sensed that citizens were discouraged from developing convictions, as if the capacity for moral judgment were too cumbersome to accompany them to a new world order.[103] Hans-Jörg Sigwart suggests Arendt steadily grew suspicious of "the integrative logic of citizenship" as defined by allocated rights and the regimes that parsed them. She grew reluctant to "rearticulat[e] political experiences" and commend action and speech "in terms of citizenship."[104] Following the allied victory in the Second World War, textbooks for civics courses and ideological conflicts with communist-allies-turned-enemies made the temptation to couple citizenship with conformity and loyalty formidable. Arendt was cutting across the grain, as was Augustine when he described the glory that was Rome as unstable and undesirable.[105] To the regimes and politically sanctioned routines created by glory hounds, he opposed apolitical possibilities inaugurated by what Sarah Stewart-Kroeker describes as the "amative and pedagogical work, initiated by the Spirit" and carried forward in "morally and aesthetically formative" "ecclesial pilgrim communit[ies]."[106] They formed a narrow path within sight of broad ways (*latas vias*) well-traveled by citizens seeking material advantage, cheering at civic pageants, and conforming their behavior to an officially approved pattern.[107] Arendt characterized pressures to conform in celebrations and censurable conduct as "deadly." It proved so in fascist regimes in the 1930s and would again prove "deadly" in the United States in and

---

[102] Agamben, *Homo Sacer*, 139–41.
[103] Arendt, "Some Questions," 744.
[104] Sigwart, *Wandering Thought*, 102.
[105] Augustine, *civ.* 10.32: *fastigio nutabundum*.
[106] Stewar-Kroeker, *Pilgrimage*, 174, referring to the institutional church rather than Augustine's intramural, experimental alternatives. I have added the plural.
[107] Augustine, *en. Ps.* 39.6.

after the 1950s, she warned, because the duress, although subtle, was dangerously "insistent."[108]

There was little room in the polis that developed from and—as Arendt came to imagine, perverted—republican sentiments she admired, little room or incentive, that is, for the activism and speech she thought critical to "the political." Freedom to act influentially and speak freely (and consequentially) was suppressed "in favor of government and obedience."[109] Before her disenchantment expressed itself in complaints about Americans' prejudices and political practices, she urged them to engage in what she called a political "enterprise" and to "insert [themselves] into the world [to] begin a story of [their] own." We have already taken account of her summons to subjects to make themselves "explicit"; she also called on them to be "tangible," to become parts of what seemed to her a "living flux of acting and speaking."[110] Arendt appeared disinclined to relinquish her view that the public realm might somehow float free of the pressures of the capitalist economy; occasionally, she parked alongside her fierce criticisms of bureaucracy her expectation that an effective civic nationalism would materialize and vaporize bureaucrats.[111] Yet she conceded that any optimal "political space" could easily be vandalized, if obsessions with consumption and with the labor required to subsidize it persisted. But the persistence could never erode some basic truths. "The life of a free [person] needed the presence of others." And, she went on, "freedom itself needed ... a place where people could come together," an "oasis," perhaps, but certainly a polis, which Arendt designated as a "political space proper."[112]

That space for action and speech did not precede the doing and discourse that filled it. For Arendt, Seyla Benhabib says, "what constitutes the political is a certain quality of the life of speech and action." And what kept that "certain quality" on tap in the world that Arendt wanted to reshape, we now know, was a willingness

---

[108] Arendt, "The Threat of Conformism," *The Commonweal*, September 24, 1954, 607–10.
[109] Canovan, *Hannah Arendt*, 148, attributing this assessment to Arendt.
[110] Arendt, *Human Condition*, 187–88.
[111] Seyla Benhabib, "Political Geographies in a Global World: Arendtian Reflections," *Social Research* 69 (2002), 542–43, 557–58 thinks so.
[112] Arendt, *On Revolution*, 21.

to begin anew (natality) and entertain equal others' opinions (plurality).[113] Might that willingness survive in an increasingly impersonal bureaucratic society? Arendt did not discount the possibility. Yet remarks scattered in her work, from start to finish, suggest that subjects can only enter "the living flux of acting and speaking" at the places, oases, counterpublics, or poleis to which we have been introduced—in sodalities or "enterprises" that offered a degree of informality, spontaneity, and ambiguity, all of which were conducive to creativity and meaningful interaction and mutual *inter-est*.[114]

Her studies of tyrannies argue that such sodalities were among the early casualties of totalitarianism. Totalitarian regimes, bent on disrupting social bonds, isolated individuals and rendered them "superfluous." Arendt claimed that even "the productive potentialities of isolation are annihilated," when regimes "destroy . . . all the space between men," stifling all creative and mutually sustaining interactions. The first work she completed on leaving Europe recognized the importance of community and plurality. "The experience of the materially and sensually given world," she stipulates, "depends on . . .. being in contact with other[s]."[115] Anya Topalski aptly paraphrases, stating that "reality check[s]" depend on sodalities permitting subjects to "train [their] imaginations to go visiting" with a latitude denied to citizens. Subjects could only then freely and effectively enter the "flux of acting and speaking" and be "tangible," as Arendt wished. Furthermore, the greater exposure their opinions and justifications were given, "the more worldly validity" they possessed.[116] Arendt's notes on Kant's *Critique of Judgment* allude to the positive outcomes of plurality and of the "visiting" to which Topalski refers. Refinements and revisions resulting from friendly exchanges of views make those views and

---

[113]Benhabib, *Reluctant Modernism*, 146. But others' equality, Arendt stipulates (*Human Condition*, 215), "is necessarily an equality of unequals" "equalized" for conversations.
[114]Arendt, *Denktagebuch*, 1:220.
[115]Arendt, *Origins of Totalitarianism*, 475–78.
[116]Anya Topolski, *Arendt, Levinas, and a Politics of Rationality* (London: Rowman and Littlefield, 2015), 48–49, 94–95.

persons who exchange them more "generally communicable" and thus politically productive.[117]

Arendt drew Aristotle's remarks on friendship into her essay on the human condition, specifying that collaboration and communication relied on colleagues' amicable relations. And the trick to forming and sustaining politically fruitful friendships was to take pleasure in diversity without seeking pleasure in domination. But "on the political scene" "hypocrisy begins to poison all human relations," Arendt proposed, nonetheless endorsing Aristotle's proviso that friendships improved friends' abilities to act, think, and speak—assisting communities as well as individuals to avoid dissembling as well as factions and to develop political virtues.[118] In the United States, however, she saw factions proliferate. Resentments eclipsed reasoning in the public realm. "The taste for political freedom" and participation there was lost. Citizens preferred to withdraw. The few, who did not, she predicted, would find no opportunity to participate substantially. Reading Arendt's later works, those few would catch her referring to citizens' consent to government conduct—and therefore citizenship and participatory democracy—as "entirely fictitious."[119]

Pariahs

She had been hopeful, as we know. But she saw that citizens' prerogatives and priorities in the twentieth century became unmoored from the expectations that induced eighteenth-century distinguished citizens' to put their signatures on the American Constitution. From the studies she undertook in the 1920s and 1930s and from her experiences as a refugee, she appreciated that pariah status came with a unique quality of perception, more realistic and invigorating than the entitlements associated with citizenship. Her essay, "We Refugees," celebrated the Jews who had abjured

---

[117] Arendt, *Lectures on Kant*, 63.
[118] Aristotle, *Nicomachean Ethics* 8.1, 1155a; Arendt, *Human Condition*, 24–25, 36–37, 214. For hypocrisy "on the political scene," see Arendt, *On Revolution*, 88.
[119] Arendt, *Crises of the Republic*, 89; Arendt, *On Revolution*, 131; Benhabib, *Reluctant Modernism*, 203–5.

"adjustment and assimilation" to become "conscious pariahs." They scooped up what she classified as "pariah qualities"—humor, humanity, and disinterested intelligence—leaving "inferiority complexes" to parvenus determined to fit in.[120] The next year, she contributed an essay on refugees to *Aufbau*, commenting on citizens' diverse reactions to refugees among them. The humor and humanity that survived the outcasts' ordeals sometimes moved their hosts to treat them reverentially, she noticed, but stateless émigrés just as often stirred suspicions—or far worse, unsubstantiated accusations that led to internments, expulsions, and extinction.[121]

Arendt experienced both the hospitality and the suspicion and enmity. After leaving Germany for Paris, she was sent to a camp for refugee women in southwestern France near Lourdes. The nutrition was adequate, but barracks morale was terrible. When the camp was evacuated, locals who opposed the Vichy government hired internees as field hands, yet Arendt remembered her friends' interminable searches for food, news, and cigarettes.[122] But afterward, she sensed what she later identified as those aforesaid admirable pariah qualities along with the refugees' resourcefulness. She referred to the latter as "a violent courage of life," the vitality of which citizens and parvenus seemed dispossessed. She concluded that, while typical parvenus contrived cloaking devices to hide unwanted traits, the "conscious pariahs" prized candor and developed an "insane optimism" "next door to despair."[123] So, when Agamben hunted for a "paradigm for the new historical consciousness," he found it in Arendt's pariah refugees.[124]

Agamben considered refugees' "violent courage" and "insane optimism" invaluable advantages. Pariahs' unpopularity saved them from servitude to the sovereign powers excluding them. One should see in the refugees' perseverance, he said, a preview of an emerging political community. Diaspora drove refugees together; precariousness prompted commiseration. Their predicament as

---

[120] Arendt, "We Refugees," in *Another Elsewhere: Writers in Exile*, ed. Marc Robinson (London: Faber and Faber, 1994), 118–19.
[121] Arendt, "Gäste aus dem Niemandsland," *Aufbau*, June 30, 1944, 15.
[122] Young-Bruehl, *Hannah Arendt*, 153–56.
[123] Arendt, "We Refugees," 113.
[124] Agamben, *Mezzi senza fine*, 20.

well as their courage called into question legislative and juridical fidgeting with concepts sanctioned by sovereign powers, including much of what was embedded in declarations of rights and usually associated with citizenship—and with sovereignty itself. The tasks ahead, he said, would require new concepts. Arendt was cautious, hoping new poleis would rediscover and restore what she took to be republican virtues. Agamben was aggressive; he feared, it seems, that any reevaluation would lead to reassertion, so he categorically called for renunciation. He looked for the political community-to-come to be new (*assolutamente nuovi che ci stanno davanti*). New politics and a new political philosophy, he said, started with the image of the refugee (*a partire da quest'unica figura*); the paladin of his new political community was Arendt's "conscious pariah."[125] Perhaps, without contending that the terms "pariah," "pilgrim," and "refugee" are synonymous, we may claim that the three should be stacked close together. For we know that Agamben hauled Arendt's pariahs from storage into his stories, and—from references scattered through her works—we know she never forgot "the bond" on which Augustine depended to hold together refugees from the terrestrial city, pilgrims to the celestial. For all three, alienation and aliens cast critical light on the prevailing political fictions of their times.[126]

Arendt's distinctions between pariahs and parvenus date to her study of Varnhagen in the 1930s, but Jeremy Adelman suggests that her work toward the end of that decade with Baroness Germaine de Rothschild in Paris was especially influential. Arendt helped monitor the baroness' philanthropy. She investigated the Jewish charities and ensured that funds were distributed as her employer wished. Adelman thinks Arendt was somewhat censorious, believing that the generous gifts were motivated more by platitudes than by principles and that the assimilated Rothschilds were unwittingly complicit in cultures that created the inequities and suffering their largesse was

---

[125] Agamben, *Mezzi senza fine*, 20–21; 68–69.
[126] Larry Ray and Maria Diemling, "Arendt's 'Conscious Pariah' and the Ambiguous Figure of the Subaltern," *European Journal of Social Theory* 19 (2016), 504–8 has Arendt's pariahs ("stateless, superfluous populations") fully engaged in struggles for rights but also sufficiently withdrawn and refusing to acquiesce in parvenu efforts to accommodate and achieve respectability.

meant to address and redress. And the complicity, of course, was regrettable. Few, if any, pariahs were positioned to assist as copiously as the parvenus, but "on the margins," they astutely poured "scorn on the happy pieties that realties hollowed out." Adelman posts his account as a tribute to Arendt, who came to feel comfortable on those margins: "it took an alien," "a stateless woman," he says, to show how tenaciously and deceptively the democratic as well as totalitarian regimes held (and hold) to shoddy principles, disincentivizing parvenus—concerned to conform—from imagining a better set. The regimes preached property, promoted security, and perpetuated the illusion of citizen participation. Pariahs, registering and passing through one crisis after another, nonetheless appear poised on the threshold of a new beginning. They come to have more robust and realistic perspectives on rights, freedoms, and life than those of parvenus.[127]

"Complicity" may be too strong a term to characterize parvenus' connections with dominant cultures' efforts to turn subjects into diffident, obedient citizens. But Agamben's complaints go beyond Arendt's. Her parvenus' benefactions were shards of what, under an altogether different set of conditions, might have composed a consciousness of collective responsibility for the persistence of inequities and injustice. For Agamben, parvenus' kind gestures simply reinforce sovereign powers' captivity of subjectivity into "forms of life" by satisfying citizens', statesmen's, philanthropists' and recipients' sense of well-being. Arendt, from Agamben's perch, accurately assessed the shortcomings of the Rothschilds' generosity, insofar as she correctly weighed the relative significance of her benefactrix's platitudes and principles. The buy-in (or complicity) for the affluent serves their self-interest. Agamben is aware that selling the disadvantaged on the legitimacy of sovereign powers and viability of prescribed forms of life poses challenges, yet he comprehends that theatrical rituals, political oratory, and opulent architectural expressions of political authority control citizens' perceptions of their states. Statist categories are sewn into the very

---

[127]Jeremy Adelman, "Pariah: Can Hannah Arendt Help us Rethink our Global Refugee Crisis?" *Wilson Quarterly* 40 (2016), accessed at https://wilsonquarterly.com/quarterly/looking-back-moving-forward/pariah-can-hannah-arendt-help-us-rethink-our-global-refugee-crisis/, January 24, 2018.

lining of business-as-usual apparel. And citizens grow incapable of thinking of political practice apart from forms dictated by resourceful sovereign powers shaping leisure as well as commerce—creating, as it suits them, emergencies or complacency—even nostalgia.[128]

Arendt also chafed at official rhetoric and rituals that called to mind republican virtues betrayed by conventional political practices, which precluded persons' "existential" engagement in speech and action in the public forum. Her essay on civil disobedience borrowed phrases from Tocqueville to congratulate "disobedients" in voluntary associations who had undertaken to "diminish the moral power of the majority." She scolded citizens and statists, overly impressed by "the grandeur of court procedure," who saw disobedients as defendants.[129] To Agamben, the apostle Paul alerted readers to see through the grandeur; his political legacy foregrounds pariahs (in this instance "the remnant") whose presence in sacred literature puts paid to obsolete notions of citizenship and democracy. The remnant is, in Agamben's scheme, messianic, and he assumes the apostle thought so as well; pariahs deliver, in two senses. They deliver citizens from their captivity by delivering a new perspective on political practice.[130]

Arendt sensed the need for deliverance in what she called "dark times" when, in 1968, she published in a single volume several tributes to variously embattled and defiant protagonists. The darkness referred not only to a series of twentieth-century mishaps and atrocities but also to normal practice in the public realm and "highly efficient talk and double talk" "camouflag[ing]" the fact that, in a specific "realm" or space, the normal "degrade[d] all truth to meaningless triviality." Arendt blamed caretakers of what she identified as "the establishment" and "the system."[131] Rosa Luxemburg was one of their nemeses. The Polish Jew who co-founded the *Spartakusbund* in Germany was "amazing[ly] clearsighted," despite the darkness, Arendt said, because, as an

---

[128] Agamben, *Homo Sacer*, 115: *costitutivamente incapace di pensare veramente nella modernitá una politica non-statuale*.
[129] Arendt, *Crises of the Republic*, 98–99. See Katherine Arens, "Hannah Arendt Translates Culture: Men in Dark Times," *Monatshefte* 108 (2016), 547–48, for Arendt's search for "existential" engagement.
[130] Agamben, *Il tempo che resta*, 58–59.
[131] Arendt, *Men in Dark Times*, viii–ix.

alien in Germany, she "was always out of step." Pariah Luxemburg strenuously opposed German nationalism during the century's first two decades. She refused to be beguiled by the nationalists' ridiculously cliché-ridden rhetoric, Arendt exclaimed, touting Luxemburg's "acute sense of [political] reality" reflected in a "brilliant" (Arendt's embroidery) analysis of how imperialism, in the service of capitalism, had deliberately forced the pace of economic development in then developing countries to subjugate their peoples and produce markets. Behind it all was the Europeans' lust to dominate.[132]

Arendt's *Dark Times* included an essay on Bertold Brecht, the dramatist, who was also "out of step," renouncing political and theatrical conventions. Brecht, she said, was particularly and effusively annoyed by the "irritating bad faith of 'prophets of the people' [and] 'voices' of history" they summoned to endorse their values. In 1918, the year before Rosa Luxemburg was murdered by paramilitary thugs—who were all but acquitted by the regime—Brecht's first major play, *Baal*, was produced. Arendt thought that Baal was the perfect deity for pariahs. As the Canaanite fertility god, Baal became, in Arendt's tribute, an emblem of the playwright's "reckless love for the earth" and of his estrangement from all political "systems" soiling it. Furthermore, as she pointed out, recollecting and perhaps recycling Brecht's love to "puncture pomposity," "Baal cannot possibly be the god of any social order."[133]

Arendt kept company with pariahs long before writing about Brecht and Luxemburg. In the 1930s, she spent time with Varnhagen. Drilling for information about anti-Semitism for her study of totalitarianism, during the 1940s, she extended her analysis of pariah and parvenu qualities to the community of assimilated Jews in Germany between the two world wars. Instead of pariahs with parvenu ambitions, she found parvenu Jews, trying to embrace the "privileges of pariahs" that their coreligionists "on the fringe of society" possessed. On Arendt's watch, the parvenu conformists achieved "equality of condition" but were resented and reviled by

---

[132] Arendt, *Men in Dark Times*, 37–43. Also, for Luxemburg's pariah status and objections to political cultures' "ready-made formulas," see Arendt's *Origins of Totalitarianism*, 148 and *On Revolution*, 256.

[133] Arendt, *Men in Dark Times*, 222–23, 230–31.

Germans who paradoxically called them out for insolence and "cringing servility." The assimilated coveted qualities outsiders appeared adept at cultivating. The anti-Semites painted parvenus as greedy; they yearned to be known, as were pariahs, for generosity. The parvenus envied the pariahs' reputation for forbearance and were desperate to disprove what Aryan critics claimed about assimilationsts' dissimulation and the abrasive "determination to push ahead" that characterized their community.[134] So, by the early 1950s, before fetching Luxemburg and Brecht, Arendt had learned enough to throw down the gauntlet: every Jew, she maintained, must decide whether to "remain a pariah . . . or become a parvenu and conformist."[135]

But she is hard to pin down. She can be counted among émigré intellectuals, outsiders-let-in, who—arguably, better than insiders— saw "narcissistic individualism" and "consumerism" eroding rather than expressing American ideals. She referred to individualism and consumerism as "dangers to democracy." Arendt did not share American political theorists' faith in the "rule of consensus." She doubted military, industrial, and political regimes would either follow that "rule" or ever tolerate genuinely new beginnings or plurality in the public realm.[136] She began looking to "organized minorities" to attract and encourage persons who prized plurality and who were unafraid to improvise radically and make new beginnings. Natality "guarantees change" and, Arendt admits, some instability, but without the death of the old and the birth of the new, she suspects, "the human race would have become extinct long ago out of unbearable boredom."[137]

For a time, in the 1940s, she was extremely enthusiastic about the farming settlements in Israel. She referred to the kibbutzim as "perhaps the most promising of all social experiments in the twentieth century," presuming that their detachment from political practices and divisions in that new and troubled nation

---

[134] Arendt, *Origins of Totalitarianism*, 54–55.

[135] Arendt, *Origins of Totalitarianism*, 66.

[136] For Arendt's dissent from American theorists on consensus, see Ferenc Feher, "The Pariah and the Citizen: On Arendt's Political Theory," *Thesis Eleven* 15 (1986), 20–28.

[137] Arendt, *Crises of the Republic*, 76–78.

enabled kibbutzniks to carry on a "quiet and effective revolution" and experiment with alternative behaviors that announced and enthroned "new values" in their new customs. Yet, as opposition grew to the two-state solution to Palestinian problems, Arendt fretted that Zionists responsible for fueling that opposition were colonizing the settlements and persuading original settlers to become ethnonationalists.[138]

But, before their "fall," did kibbutzim remind her of Augustine's alternative, experimental communities? If the kibbutznicks valued detachment, as Arendt originally supposed, she might well have connected their intention with what she saw as Augustine's: the creation of bonds between people that were "strong enough to replace the world." But she must have been of two minds by the late 1950s. One page of her *Human Condition* is skeptical about Augustine's chances to "found a public realm," yet the very next refers to the convents, for which he supplied the impulse and the rules in the fifth century, as the "only communities in which the principle of charity as a political device was ever tried."[139] They were close to what Arendt commended as "counterworlds." She admired them, as Agamben does, yet her terms of endearment were more subdued than his are. For, despite having identified charity "as a political device," she asserted that Christianity "constituted within the world a totally new, religiously defined public space, which, although public, was *not* political."[140] Shuffling Arendt's statements to come up with a coherent position is quite a challenge. Would she, if called to account, reply that "the principle of charity" had been "tried"—yet failed? Probably not, because she did imagine friendships and forgiveness worked to minimize the risk that plurality would spur disharmony and acrimony.

---

[138] For the first hints of regret, see Arendt, "Peace or Armistice in the Near East," *Review of Politics* 12 (1950), 74–76; for "new values" and "the quiet revolution," see Arendt's essay "To Save the Jewish Homeland," first published in *Commentary* in 1948 and reprinted in Arendt, *The Jewish Writings*, ed. Jerome Kohn and Ron H. Feldman (New York: Shocken, 2007), 395–96.
[139] Arendt, *Human Condition*, 53–54.
[140] *Promise of Politics*, 139, emphasis added.

Arendt, Augustine, Agamben: Concluding remarks

Friendships worked, but Arendt thought Socrates made a mistake trying to turn citizens into friends. It was a fool's errand. Envy and animosities typically prevailed in political cultures. Socrates failed to foresee the "agonal spirit" that "was to bring the Greek city-states to ruin"; the "commonness of the[ir] political world," Arendt said, "was constituted only by the walls of the city and the boundaries of its laws. It was not seen or experienced in the relationships between the citizens." Arendt's Socrates, on Plato's stage, finally offered that complaint. It came as an epiphany of sorts that protest or complaint was central to the philosopher's political function. Arendt added a second function: articulating alternatives, which proposed that, on smaller scale, friendships transformed people into "partners in a common world." Friendships became common bonds, forming communities. Much as Augustine in his sermons, correspondence, and *City*, she saw that justice and civic pride were more fragile bonds than affection. Predictably, friendships also lubricated efforts to inventory and reshape perspectives about one's views and oneself—as well as to become well informed about alternatives from multiple sources in one's community. "That in ... dialogue" friends come to understand the "truth inherent in [an]other's opinion," Arendt wrote, was "the political element in friendship"; seeing the world through friends' eyes was "the political kind of insight par excellence."[141]

Enigmatically, when she theorized thinking, Arendt implied it was sufficient to keep company with oneself, as if her anthems to plurality had never been scripted. But Judith Butler persuasively argues that, even when Arendt wrote about "silent," "solitary," "interior" discourses, plurality was assumed, and others were present. "A form of enmeshment" with others "becomes the condition of [one's] own individuation." Or, as John Douglas Macready says, "collaborative thinking and dialogue" reveal "the who" hidden from oneself and, therefore, excellently outfit a self

---

[141] Arendt, "Philosophy and Politics," *Social Research* 71 (2004), 435–37.

for self-reflection. Plurality, Arendt pronounced, was "the law of the earth."[142]

Plurality fostered friendships, and its contributions to what Arendt valued as action and discourse depended on them. Still, she mistrusted poleis held together by "mere feeling."[143] She remembered that King Solomon, "who certainly knew something of political action," asked God for "an understanding heart," but she promptly specified that the "faculty" he prayed for was "as far removed from sentimentality as . . . from paperwork." This may be but a slender concession to affect, nonetheless, together with the roles Arendt assigned to friendships and forgiveness in sustaining alternative poleis, it suggests we may be justified supplying the "com" to the passion that, for her, brought the "revelatory quality of speech and action . . . to the fore where people are *with* others and neither for nor against them . . . in sheer togetherness."[144] To the extent that envy and malice infiltrate and polarize public forums, this "neither for nor against" and "sheer togetherness" seem to summon or conjure something utopian. Arendt displaced sovereignty with plurality and played the pariah among pundits who refused to relinquish their obsessions with the "political theology of sovereignty." Her outsider status in the United States had relatively benign consequences; pariahs, who were and later became casualties of such obsessions, suffered terrible losses, particularly as inequities and humiliations (or growing globalization) eroded sovereign powers' sense of power. Ayten Gündoğdu, adopting what she calls an "Arendtian perspective," is critical of sovereignty's compensatory strategies that introduce "a new security discourse," which refers to the presence of unwanted émigrés as "a permanent crisis or state of emergency." Gündoğdu deploys Wendy Brown's exquisite analysis

---

[142] Arendt, *The Life of the Mind: Thinking* (New York: Harcourt, Brace, Jovanovich, 1978), 19–20. Macready, "Hannah Arendt and the Political Meaning of Human Dignity," 404–5, 411–12; Judith Butler, "Arendt: Thinking Cohabitation and the Dispersion of Sovereignty," in *Sovereignty in Ruins: A Politics of Crisis*, ed. George Edmundson and Klaus Mladek (Durham: Duke University Press, 2018), 227, 232–34.

[143] See, for example, Singer, "Thinking Friendship with and against Hannah Arendt," 12.

[144] Arendt, *Human Condition*, 179–80, emphasis in the original, and Arendt, "Understanding and Politics," 391, for Solomon's request.

of "waning sovereignty" putting pariahs on notice.[145] Yet Agamben does so as well, circulating his signature suspicions about sovereign powers' seemingly perpetual recourse to—and citizens' mindless acquiescence in—a "state of exception" wherein crisis purports to justify persecuting pariahs, and the ability to persecute gives the illusion of restored potency. Stringent measures and strategic fictions create what Agamben calls space without law in which sovereign power, under the pretext of applying law, preserves and rationalizes its existence in a juridical void, *ad alcun costo*, at any cost.[146]

Agamben's arraignment of sovereign power might have gone relatively unnoticed, save for gatherings in some quarters where political theory regularly gets sifted, were it not for fears associated with terrorism, displaced persons, irregular internments, and all-too-comprehensive surveillance in the early twenty-first century. Sovereignty now seems sinister, and Agamben's remarks seem timely. He often comes off as extreme, professing that sovereign powers do just about anything to preserve their right to do anything to anyone (*di fare qualunque a chiunque*).[147] But mention of Guantanamo Bay, Abu Ghraib, the Calais "jungle," and Rohingya refugee camps tends to yield credibility to Agamben's narratives about sovereign powers' dehumanization—and exploitation—of many unfortunates. As William Rasch says, Agamben's sovereign "plunges us" into brutalities from which Thomas Hobbes's sovereign was to have rescued us. Hence, Rasch continues, "embracing the political," is not only an unmistakable symptom of citizens' captivity but, "in Agamben's eyes, can only be seen as . . . sin."[148] We now know Agamben's alternative to that embrace: a deactivation of protocols

---

[145] Ayten Gündoğdu, *Rightlessness in an Age of Rights: Hannah Arendt and the Contemporary Struggles of Migrants* (Oxford: Oxford University Press, 2015), 92–93, 108–9. Also consult Wendy Brown, *Walled States, Waning Sovereignty* (New York: Zone Books, 2014), 85–90, 119–25 and, for "the political theology of sovereignty," Benhabib, "Political Geographies in a Global World," 563.
[146] Agamben, *Stato di eccezione*, 66–67: *il vuoto giuridico che è in questione nello stato di eccezione sembra assolutamente impensabile per il diritto; dall'altra, questo impensabile riveste però per l'ordine giuridico una rilevanza strategica decisiva, che si tratta appunto di non lasciarsi ad alcun costo sfuggire.*
[147] Agamben, *Homo sacer*, 112.
[148] William Rasch, "From Sovereign Ban to Banning Sovereignty," in *Giorgio Agamben: Sovereignty and Life*, ed. Matthew Calarco and Steven DeCaroli (Stanford: Stanford University Press, 2007), 101–7.

permitting the maneuvers of sovereignty in the state of exception to pass as law. But deactivation is not an invitation to indolence. To the critics who catch a scent of nihilism in Agamben's messianic deactivation or nullification, he responds with a distinction. Nihilism is imperfect; it nullifies laws and customs and retains the nothing (*il nulla*) as an infinitely deferred plausibility. Messianic deactivations, he argues, citing Walter Benjamin, achieve something resembling redemption and prepare for a moral rearmament in "new politics" by striking down the nothing (*rovescio del nulla*). Much as Augustine located emancipation and deactivation *intus* or *in cordis*, in the hearts of soon-to-be pilgrims—God's gifts of faith and love leading the unrepentant to repentance—Agamben's overcoming both sovereignty and *il nulla* occurs in dispositions.[149] And the results of their rehabilitation and reorientation are a happy life (*vita felice*) and a sufficient life (*vita sufficiente*) over which sovereign powers and the spectacle they and their media and marketplace accomplices stage have no power.[150]

But, because Augustine gave grudging endorsement to participation in public life and supposed that one must take protocols as one finds them—without turning them, as Agamben would, to different uses—Agamben probably would have judged what the bishop defined as an emancipation incomplete. He welcomed Augustine's conventual community as one acceptable, commendable, alternative form of life, but he seems uninformed about Augustine's previous efforts to assemble his colleagues in communities devoted to contemplation and conversation.[151] No doubt, Agamben, had he known of them, would have said they placed insufficient emphasis on inoperativity and potency, though, as Augustine clarified their purposes, they look strikingly compatible with Agamben's objectives: to contemplate and implement a happy life apart from biopolitical conventions and independent of the topoi or forms of life sanctioned by sovereign powers. Agamben's project, Kevin Attell explains, is "to halt the juridical machine by exposing the void that lies at the center of its articulating

---

[149] Compare Agamben, "Il Messia e il sovrano," 19 with Augustine, ep. 138.13-14.
[150] Agamben, *Mezzi senza fine*, 91.
[151] See Agamben, *Altissima povertà*, 41–42.

mechanism."[152] Augustine thought the void had been filled in his time by a lust for domination and glory, and the previous chapter here explored how he refined that idea and studiously substantiated it with historical details. From his pilgrims' pariah perspective, the world was a grim place. The same could be said of perspectives that Agamben attributes to (or bestows on) his refugees. But Agamben concludes with a challenge that attends and follows the refugees' deactivation of prevailing protocols. He would have them find new uses for the juridical machine—and for law—opening a passage to justice.[153] Neither he nor Augustine suggested significant structural changes would follow; neither anticipated what we might recognize as a comprehensive renovation.

No escape was on offer for either. Augustine was more specific than Agamben (*inter malos est; nec recedere a malis potest*), although both would have readers return to realities remote from the ideal. Augustine was also more attentive to the consolations that constituted what was, from his perspective, the happy and sufficient life, consolations preceded by—and conditional upon—one's confession of insufficiency, namely the love of and for God present (with faith) in the hearts of pilgrims to the celestial city sojourning on earth and paying love forward in compassion for others.[154]

This was too much love for Arendt. The risk was that compassionate individuals might lose themselves—or "fuse" themselves—and diminish or obliterate the very differences between personalities and perspectives that made plurality productive. Arendt appreciated that love had been as vital for Augustine as humility. Those two virtues were checks against arrogance that—spiking—killed the soul's chances to experience God's love and, consequently, to return to God. Whereas, for the Augustine who inhabited Arendt's dissertation, *caritas* consummated (*vollzieht*) an individual's existence, consummation required a dollop of self-

---

[152] Kevin Attell, *Giorgio Agamben: Beyond the Threshold of Deconstruction* (New York: Fordham University Press, 2014), 164.
[153] Agamben, *Stato di eccezione*, 83: *ad aprire un varco verso giustizia*.
[154] Augustine, *en. Ps.* 119.6-7 and *en. Ps.* 149.5. Love is also, for Agamben, the consolation that opens possibilities for communities of singularities whose affections do not depend on the predicates of those loved or on conditions of belonging. See Agamben, *La communità che vienne*, 3–4.

renunciation.¹⁵⁵ And there was no place for asceticism in the new politics sketched in her later political theory. But she snatched another Augustine who helped her defend the ground she occupied early on and never relinquished, the proposition that self-discovery and self-development or, in her terms, "self-extension" only could be realized in dialogue with others—that is, in some sort of polis. She could not disregard the ascetic Augustine; rules for, and practices in, his alternative poleis definitely foregrounded humility and retained an emphasis on self-denial. Still, years after completing her dissertation, she revisited the evidence she accumulated for her undertaking and credited Augustine with having undermined earlier Christianity's "anti-political attitude." Forgetting fourth-century theologians' enthusiasms for their empire, Arendt presumed that all the faithful were concerned to save themselves and eager to let earthly poleis perish. She believed the faith's "anti-political impulses" would have prevailed, had it not been for Augustine—a different Augustine from the one she blamed for having created apolitical spaces—an Augustine who morphed into Arendt's "greatest theorist of Christian politics." He stepped up to correct Christians' individualism. He continued to "immortalize" souls yet situated them in communities on earth (on pilgrimage) and in heaven. He continued to think that poleis and politicians in time were engaged in ignominious pursuits of glory. For Arendt's Augustine, those pursuits did not cease being odious perversions of politics; her Augustine read back into Christianity the togetherness its sacred literature about love prescribed for "the plurality of men, one of the prerequisites of political life."¹⁵⁶

To promote plurality and preserve its contributions to political discourse and practice, Arendt looked for new beginnings in alternative poleis, "bring[ing] the pariah to center stage as her more important model of the political actor."¹⁵⁷ She did not explicitly refer to the alternative communities, *neben und gegen*, Augustine proposed, even though she borrowed a passage from his *City of God*

---

¹⁵⁵Arendt, *Liebesbegriff*, 66: *sie hat als creatura auf sich selbst verzicht getan*.
¹⁵⁶Arendt, *Between Past and Future*, 72–74.
¹⁵⁷Ring, "The Pariah as Hero," 444–46 thinks of the pariah as hero of Arendt's "moveable polis."

on new births or beginnings for her notion of natality.[158] Still, after her decades-long disenchantment with the political practices in her adopted country, she wrote Karl Jaspers that she was returning to the doctoral dissertation he had supervised, looking to translate it into English. Forty years had passed, but Arendt said she recognized herself in the text (*erkenne ich mich*), a remark that could mean she had come around to see that Augustine's alternatives, just as her "oases," *neben und gegen*, had not been altogether unworldly "places of relaxation but [were] life-giving sources that let us live in the desert without becoming reconciled to it."[159]

The desert remained a desert. Reformists' efforts seemed incapable of greening it, and citizens were stranded there. Pilgrims, refugees, and pariahs—according to Augustine, Agamben, and Arendt, respectively—could see as much. Augustine's communitarian alternative was the best defined of the three proposed remedies or substitutes. His harbor imagery, as we know, permitted an outlet into and an inlet from the troubled waters of this wicked world. For isolation was not an option. Agamben's is the least well-defined alternative and can hardly be called communitarian. Other captives never figure prominently in his summonses to deactivate conventional protocols and practices. One could argue that his calls for new uses of the sovereign powers' apparatuses have no ascertainable social consequences.[160] Communication rather than community is critical, yet alternative whatevers, he says, will participate in a "new political history" and will form the community-to-come. It will be non-statist (*non-stato*), opposed to the state—*neben und gegen*—and opposing an emancipated humanity to the concept of citizen. Agamben promises something unrepresentable will somehow be shared (*co-appartengano*), something that will give a sense of belonging without stipulating conditions for belonging or asserting a representable identity.[161]

---

[158] See, for example, Augustine, *civ.* 12.20 and Arendt, *Human Condition*, 177. For well-deserved criticism of Arendt's appropriation, see Vorwinckel, *Geschichtsbegriff*, 337–38.

[159] Arendt, *Promise of Politics*, 202–3. See Arendt, *Briefwechsel*, 658, for her letter to Jaspers.

[160] Agamben, *Il tempo che resta*, 38. I take exception to that argument at length in my forthcoming *On Agamben, Community, Grace, and Missing Links*.

[161] Agamben, *La communità che viene*, 58–59: *co-appartengano senza una rappresentabile condizione di appartenenza*.

So, in so many respects, Agamben is *sui generis*, but that has not kept this study from enrolling him in the choir of political theorists for whom "non-conformism [is] the overriding feature of . . . communities formed in opposition to modernity."[162] Arguably, Arendt should be reserved an honored seat in its stalls. She, too, privileged communication and let communities take shape (or not) around it. And she was nearly as stingy as Agamben with specifics. Acting and speaking were conditions for belonging—forgiveness and promise keeping came later into play—and her alternative poleis are possible wherever an "organization of the people . . . arises out of acting and speaking together" to make new beginnings.[163]

If we set aside the various levels of integration Augustine, Arendt, and Agamben required (or required to be disavowed) for the alternatives proffered by each of our three to "arise"—*neben und gegen*—we may be grateful to them for having alerted us to the need for radical innovations and for having identified and savaged the spectacles, selfishness, prejudices, powers, and lusts that make meaningful renovation impractical. The conceit of this study is that the legacies of these three critics and visionaries are well served by placing them in conversation.

---

[162]Delanty, *Community*, 24.
[163]Arendt, *Human Condition*, 198.

FURTHER READING

Abbott, Matthew, *The Figure of this World: Agamben and the Question of Political Ontology*. Edinburgh: Edinburgh University Press, 2014.
Alici, Luigi (ed.), *I conflitti religiosi nella scena pubblica: Agostino a confronto con manichei e donatisti*. Rome: Città Nuova, 2015.
Arendt, Hannah, *Der Liebesbegriff bei Augustin: Versuch einer philosophischen Interpretation*. Berlin: Springer, 1929.
Arnold, Kathleen, *Arendt, Agamben, and the Issue of Hyper Legality: In Between the Prisoner-Stateless Nexus*. London: Routledge, 2018.
Attell, Kevin, *Giorgio Agamben: Beyond the Threshold of Deconstruction*. New York: Fordham University Press, 2014.
Benhabib, Seyla, *Exile, Statelessness, and Migration: Playing Chess with History from Hannah Arendt to Isaiah Berlin*. Princeton: Princeton University Press, 2018.
Bernstein, Richard J., *Why Read Hannah Arendt Now*. Cambridge: Polity, 2018.
Blanchard, W. Scott, "Forms of Power, Forms of Life: Agamben's Franciscan Turn," *New Literary History* 46 (2015), 525–48.
Breyfogle, Todd, *Reading Augustine: On Creativity, Liberty, Love, and the Beauty of the Law*. New York: Bloomsbury, 2017.
Brown, Peter, *Augustine of Hippo: A Biography*, 2nd ed. Berkeley: University of California Press, 2000.
Canovan, Margaret, *Hannah Arendt: A Reinterpretation of Her Political Thought*. Cambridge: Cambridge University Press, 1992.
Clair, Joseph, *Discerning the Good in the Letters and Sermons of Augustine*. Oxford: Oxford University Press, 2016.
Colebrook, Claire and Maxwell, Jason, *Agamben*. Cambridge: Polity, 2016.
Conybeare, Catherine, *The Irrational Augustine*. Oxford: Oxford University Press, 2006.
Dodaro, Robert, *Christ and the Just Society in the Thought of Augustine*. Cambridge: Cambridge University Press, 2004.
Dunning, Benjamin H., *Aliens and Sojourners: Self as Other in Early Christian Society*. Philadelphia: University of Pennsylvania Press, 2009.

Durantaye, Leland de la, *Giorgio Agamben: A Critical Introduction*. Stanford: Stanford University Press, 2009.
Geulen, Eva, Kauffmann, Kai, and Mein, Georg (eds.), *Hannah Arendt und Giorgio Agamben: Parallelen, Perspektiven, Kontroversen*. Munich: Fink, 2008.
Gregory, Eric. *Politics and the Order of Love: An Augustinian Ethic of Democratic Citizenship*. Chicago: University of Chicago Press, 2008.
Gündoğdu, Ayten, *Rightlessness in an Age of Rights: Hannah Arendt and the Contemporary Struggles of Migrants*. Oxford: Oxford University Press, 2015.
Herb, Karlfriedrich, Morgenstern, Katherin, and Gebhardt, Mareika (eds.), *Raum und Zeit: Denkformen des Politischen bei Hannah Arendt*. Frankfurt am Main: Campus, 2014.
Hollingworth, Miles, *The Pilgrim City: St Augustine of Hippo and His Innovation in Political Thought*. London: Clark, 2010.
Hombert, Pierre-Marie, *Gloria Gratiae: Se glorifier en Dieu, principe et fin de la théologie augustinienne de la grâce*. Paris: Institut d'Études Augustiniennes, 1996.
King, Richard H., *Arendt and America*. Chicago: University of Chicago Press, 2015.
Kishik, David, *The Power of Life: Agamben and the Coming Politics*. Stanford: Stanford University Press, 2012.
Kotsko, Adam and Salzani, Carlo (eds.), *Agamben's Philosophical Lineage*. Edinburgh: Edinburgh University Press, 2017.
Lechte, John, *Bare Life and Ways of Life*. London: Bloomsbury, 2018.
Lechte, John and Newman, Saul, *Agamben and the Politics of Human Rights: Statelessness, Images, Violence*. Edinburgh: Edinburgh University Press, 2013.
Lee, Gregory W., "Republics and their Loves: Rereading *City of God* 19," *Modern Theology* 27 (2011), 553–81.
Maier, Franz Georg, *Augustin und das antike Rom*. Stuttgart: Kohlhammer, 1955.
Marafioti, Domenico, "Comme leggere il *De civitate Dei*," *Augustinianum* 53 (2013), 441–67.
Mathewes, Charles, *The Republic of Grace: Augustinian Thoughts for Dark Times*. Grand Rapids: Eerdmans, 2010.
Mayer, Cornelius (ed.), *Augustinus: Recht und Gewalt*. Würzburg: Echter, 2010.
McLoughlin, Daniel (ed.), *Agamben and Radical Politics*. Edinburgh: Edinburgh University Press, 2016.
Nixon, Jon, *Hannah Arendt and the Politics of Friendship*. London: Bloomsbury, 2015.

Prozorov, Sergei, *Agamben and Politics: A Critical Introduction*. Oxford: Oxford University Press, 2014.
Salzani, Carlo, *Introduzione a Giorgio Agamben*. Genoa: Il Melangolo, 2013.
Schwartz, Jonathan Peter, *Arendt's Judgment: Freedom, Responsibility, and Citizenship*. Philadelphia: University of Pennsylvania Press, 2016.
Sigwart, Hans-Jörg, *The Wandering Thought of Hannah Arendt*. New York: Palgrave Macmillan, 2015.
Stewart-Kroeker, Sarah, *Pilgrimage as Moral and Aesthetic Formation in Augustine's Thought*. Oxford: Oxford University Press, 2017.
Stock, Brian, *The Integrated Self: Augustine, the Bible, and Ancient Thought*. Philadelphia: University of Pennsylvania Press, 2017.
Vowinckel, Annette, *Geschichtsbegriff und historisches Denken bei Hannah Arendt*. Cologne: Böhlau, 2001.
Wetzel, James (ed.), *Augustine's 'City of God': A Critical Guide*. Cambridge: Cambridge University Press, 2012.
Whyte, Jessica, *Catastrophe and Redemption: The Political Thought of Giorgio Agamben*. Albany: State University of New York Press, 2013.
Young-Bruehl, Elisabeth, *Hannah Arendt: For Love of the World*, 2nd ed. New Haven: Yale University Press, 2004.

INDEX

Abu Ghraib 142
Achilles 122
Actium 68
Adelman, Jeremy 134
Adeodatus 18
Adrianople 79
Agamben, Giorgio
  on Augustine 13, 33–7
  criticisms of political
    culture 4–5, 27–47,
    109–10, 127–8, 143–5
  on Hannah Arendt 133–4,
    109, 147
  messianic expectations 31–2,
    35, 44, 51–2, 116, 136, 143
Alexander the Great 75
Alici, Luigi, 38
Altar of Victory 66
Alypius, bishop of Thagaste 62,
  77
Ambrose, bishop of Milan 55–6,
  93
Apringius 2–3, 9
Arendt, Hannah
  assessment of American
    republic 101–8, 111–12,
    117–18
  on Augustine 99–106, 121,
    139, 144–6
  disenchantment of 101–2,
    106–12, 123–7, 132, 138,
    146
  pariah and parvenu cultures
    117, 126–7, 132–42

Aristotle 28, 132
Attell, Kevin 143–4
Augustine, bishop of Hippo
    Regius. *See also*
    Cassiciacum; Thagaste
  criticisms of political
    culture 1–13, 24–7, 63–76,
    113–14, 127–8
  on idolatry 75–81
Augustus, emperor 66
Aurelius, bishop of Carthage 62
Auschwitz 32, 128

Badiou, Alain 49–51
BeDuhn, Jason David 56–7
Benhabib, Seyla 130–1
Benjamin, Walter 47, 143
"biopolitical machine"
    (Agamben) 28–31, 143–4
Bolshevism 108
Brecht, Bertold 137–38
Brown, Peter 62
Brown, Wendy 141–2
Burns, Daniel 126
"business of Babylon"
    (Augustine) 7–8, 11,
    15–16, 26, 53, 80
Butler, Judith 140

Caecilian, Roman statesman
    1–5, 9
Caelestius, Pelagian theorist
    59–60
Canovan, Margaret 125–6

INDEX

Carthage, Council of (411) 9–10, 92
Cassiciacum 14–18, 21, 36, 51, 69
Catilina, Lucius Sergius 69–73
Cicero, Marcus Tullius 63, 69, 71, 79
citizenship 1–2, 5, 43–5, 127–32, 140
Clair, Joseph 24 n.72
Constantine, emperor 6, 63

Debord, Guy 35, 50
Delanty, Gerard 44
de Rothschild, Germaine 134–5
de Saint-Just, Louis Antoine 106
Descartes, René 115
de Tocqueville, Alexis 136
Diocesan courts 6–7
Dodaro, Robert 25 n.75, 63–4, 73, 95
Donatism 7–10, 25–6, 56, 91–3, 96
Dunning, Benjamin 83

Edkins, Jenny 52
Eichmann, Adolf 109
Ernesti, Jörg 94
Evodius 18, 96

faith 7, 12, 37–9, 89, 96
fascism and totalitarianism 30–3, 42–3, 100–1, 108–11, 119–20, 131. *See also* nazism
Fichte, Johann Gottlieb 117
Firmus, proconsular legate 93
Fontrevault 53
Foucault, Michel 28, 37, 47
friendship 14–15, 121–2, 139–41

Geulen, Eva 128
Gnosticism 29

grace 7, 39–40, 58–62, 86–7
Gregory, Eric 1 n.1, 104
Guantanamo 142
Gündoğdu, Ayten 141–2

Hannibal Barca 14–15, 68–9
Herodotus 122
Hitler, Adolf 31, 108
Hobbes, Thomas 142
Hollingworth, Miles 92–3
Hombert, Pierre-Marie 62, 73–4, 84 n.131
Homer 122
Honorius, emperor 9
Horn, Christoph 93, 95
Humiliati 52

Jaspers, Karl 99, 105, 107–8, 123
Jefferson, Thomas 104–5, 108
Julian of Eclanum, Pelagian theorist 60–1, 71, 90–1

Kant, Immanuel 122, 131–2
Keedus, Liisi 123–4
kibbutzim 138–9
King, Richard 117

Lagouanère, Jérôme 39–40
Lamb, Michael 1 n.1
Lechte, John 127
Lee, Gregory 81
Lettieri, Gaetano 85
Licentius, 14–15, 26
Livy, Titus 63, 67–8
Luxemburg, Rosa 136–8

Macedonius, Roman statesman 1, 25–6, 58
McGowan, John 127
MacIntyre, Alasdair 42, 45
Madison, James 107
Magrini, James 120
Maier, Franz Georg 71

Manichees and Manichaeism 20–3, 55–61, 70, 87, 96, 126
Marafioti, Domenico 88
Marcellinus, Roman statesman 1–6, 9–11, 26, 64, 92–5
Marinus, Roman commander 2–5
Marius, Caius, Roman consul 65–7, 70, 73
Markus, Robert 24 n.72
martyrs and martyrdom 25–6, 72, 82–4, 89, 96–7
Marxism 115, 119–20
Massignon, Louis 46
Mathewes, Charles 1, 41, 43
mendicants 34–6, 52–3, 95
Milbank, John 92–3
Mills, Catherine 128
Mills, C. Wright 41–2, 112
Mommsen, Theodor 110
Mourad, Ronney 33 n.97

natality (Arendt) 100, 115–25, 138–9, 145–6
nazism 30–3, 137–8
Nebridius 15, 23
Nebuchadnezzar 10–11
Newman, Saul 127
Nicaea, Council of 61
Nietzsche, Friedrich 13, 118
Nixon, Jon 121
Norbert of Xanten 52–3

O'Donovan, Oliver 26–7, 31
Optatus, bishop of Thamugadi 9 n.24
Orosius 5–6

pagans and paganism 29, 64–7, 70–1, 88, 90, 96, 126
Paine, Thomas 105, 108

Pelagianism 19–21, 39–40, 56–62, 86–91, 114, 126
pilgrims and refugees 8–9, 13–40, 72–6, 80, 96–7, 114–15, 119, 146–7
Pindar 47
Pizzolato, Luigi Franco 20
Plato and Platonism 56, 105, 124, 140
Praemonstratensians 53
Proba 18–19
Prozorov, Sergei 44

Ratzinger, Joseph (Pope Benedict XVI) 8
Riesman, David 119
Ring, Jennifer 113
Robert of Arbrissel 52–3
Robespierre, Maximilien 106–7
Romanianus 14
RosàsTosas, Mar 120
Rousseau, Jean Jacques 102

Saguntum and Saguntines 67–9, 73
Sallust (Gaius Sallustius Crispus) 63–5, 69–71, 79
Schmitt, Carl 47, 50
Shklar, Judith 115
Sigwart, Hans-Jörg 119, 129
Socrates 140
Spartakusbund 108, 136–7
Stalin, Joseph 108, 115
"state of exception" (Agamben) 27, 31–3
Stewart-Kroeker, Sarah 16, 20, 129
Symmachus, Quintus Aurelius 66–7

Tertullian 104
Thagaste 16–18, 21, 26, 36, 51, 100

Theodosius I, emperor 6, 11, 93–5
Thucydides 122
Tiananmen Square 52
Topalski, Anya 131
Trygetius 69

Valens, emperor 79
Varnhagen, Rahel 105–6, 117, 34

Varro Marcus Terrentius 63, 79
Vergil (Publius Vergilius Maro) 81–2
Vichy France 133

Zaretsky, Eli 116, 119–20
zionism 106, 115–16, 138–9